At Issue

Extreme Sports

Other Books in the At Issue Series:

At Issue

Extreme Sports

Janel D. Ginn, Book Editor

GREENHAVEN PRESS

An imprint of Thomson Gale, a part of The Thomson Corporation

Detroit • New York • San Francisco • New Haven, Conn. • Waterville, Maine • London

THOMSON

────────✱────────™

GALE

Christine Nasso, *Publisher*
Elizabeth Des Chenes, *Managing Editor*

© 2008 The Gale Group.

Star logo is a trademark and Gale and Greenhaven Press are registered trademarks used herein under license.

For more information, contact:
Greenhaven Press
27500 Drake Rd.
Farmington Hills, MI 48331-3535
Or you can visit our Internet site at http://www.gale.com

LIBRARY OF CONGRESS CATALOGING-IN-PUBLICATION DATA

Extreme sports / Janel D. Ginn, book editor.
    p. cm. -- (At issue)
Includes bibliographical references and index.
ISBN-13: 978-0-7377-2296-3 (hardcover)
ISBN-13: 978-0-7377-2297-0 (pbk.)
 1. Extreme sports. 2. Risk-taking (Psychology). I. Ginn, Janel, 1983-
GV749.7.E985 2008
796.04'6--dc22
                                                    2007026033

ISBN-10: 0-7377-2296-7 (hardcover)
ISBN-10: 0-7377-2297-5 (pbk.)

Printed in the United States of America
10 9 8 7 6 5 4 3 2 1

Contents

Introduction

Over the past few decades, a paradigmatic shift occurred in athletic activities. Extreme sports gave birth to events from surfing to snowboarding to cliff jumping, gaining momentum with a growing fan base for each new recreational activity. Many sports evolved from individual leisure pursuits to competitions between those who dared to push the boundaries of their bodies and gravity.

With the creation of the X Games, increased coverage from television networks, and a gradual entrance into the Olympic spotlight, popularity of extreme sports among fans and participants soared. Extreme athletes embraced their reputation as daredevils, creating a radical subculture centered on their ground-breaking sports.

As athletes gain experience and push their abilities to untested limits, controversial questions continue to rise. Are extreme sports more dangerous than traditional sports? Can new sports such as "extreme ironing" really be considered athletic events, or are they temporary fads created by individuals seeking popularity? Should the Olympics continue adding extreme sports to its roster? Emotions and facts support arguments on both sides of each issue.

Medical evidence concludes the number of injuries suffered by athletes is no higher in extreme sports than traditional sports. However, physicians are quick to note the types of injuries received in an extreme sport are often more severe and inflict greater long-term damage on a body. Despite these statistics, most athletes insist the thrill of the activity is worth the health risk, even though an alarming number of individuals possess no health insurance to cover the serious injuries associated with extreme sports.

Perhaps this nonchalant attitude toward danger is expected from the stereotypical extreme sport enthusiast: a teenager with an endless appetite for thrills, but lacking in common sense. However, extreme sports are gaining respect from some surprising advocates. This year, the U.S. military opened the Center for the Intrepid in San Antonio. The rehabilitation facility incorporates several extreme sports, including rappelling and (simulated) surfing as part of comprehensive therapy for wounded veterans. Patients and therapists consider extreme sports an integral step in healing physical injuries, as well as building the confidence essential to emotional and mental recovery of combat veterans.

Many schools are now incorporating extreme sports into their physical education curriculum. This movement marks a significant change in the learning objectives for students: from the values of teamwork and competition to a new emphasis on the importance of finding exercise enjoyable and celebrating personal improvement and achievement. Teachers and administrators hope this new direction in physical education encourages children to pursue an activity they enjoy into their adulthood. Success will be measured by whether the percentage of overweight Americans declines in coming years.

Even business professionals want in on the extreme sports craze. A growing number make reservations for retreats and weekend getaways to learn everything from water skiing to sky diving. Many find the exhilaration a refreshing change from the stress of the office and pursue extreme activities in their free time to combat the burn out they often experience from their jobs.

Extreme sports are also used as a way to connect at-risk teens with mentors. Surfing, water skiing, or snowboarding can provide students with alternatives to illegal activities, and advocates insist it reduces gang violence and drug abuse. In areas without nearby access to large bodies of water or mountains, organizations raise funds to sponsor underprivileged kids on trips. The opportunity to participate in extreme sports and see another part of the country often opens their eyes to their own potential and gives them hope regarding the future.

Criticism of extreme sports is as strong as support, even within the athletic community. Some "traditional" athletes argue that extreme sports are not real sports, because the emphasis is not on teamwork or competition. Individuals who worked to establish the extreme sports community worry that up-and-coming athletes are blinded by the desire for fame and fortune. If competitors idolize the media spotlight and pursue contracts for product endorsement, the extreme sports community will lose the rebellious image that separated it from traditional athletics.

Safety concerns are a constant issue. States across the country are enacting a variety of measures in an attempt to reduce injuries and fatalities, and proposals for more restrictions continue to reach local and state legislators. Most parents take matters into their own hands, requiring their children to wear proper safety equipment or attend classes or private lessons for safety education, or they prohibit their children from participating in any extreme sports to avoid risk of injury.

Success for extreme sports through integration into the Olympics, promotion from a barrage of advertisers, and a growing fan base through ESPN's televised coverage of the X Games and other events is tempered by opposition from many concerned parents, physicians, and legislators. Thus far, extreme sports enthusiasts continue achieving their goals of breaking the "sports mold" and creating controversy, pushing the limits of death-defying stunts, and portraying themselves as athletic mavericks. It remains to be seen whether extreme sports will continue to compete with traditional sports or will lose support and fade into obscurity.

1

Extreme Sports Pose No More Danger than Traditional Sports

Greg Connors

Greg Connors is a sports reporter for the Buffalo News *in Buffalo, New York.*

Perceptions of the risks surrounding extreme sports aren't supported by statistics. Most individuals who pursue non-traditional sports are not reckless or trying to cheat death, and with proper safety equipment, "extreme" athletes face the same likelihood of injury as those involved in traditional recreation.

BMX cyclist and X Games veteran Mat Hoffman has undergone 16 operations. Another BMX master, Syracuse native Dave Mirra, lost his spleen after crashing on his bicycle. Motocross daredevil Carey Hart has suffered some 50 broken bones.

Meanwhile, Hamburg's own X Games competitor, 20-year-old Katie Ketchum, reports just one strained ligament in her five years as an in-line skater.

While each sport is different, as well as each individual, statistics show that the so-called extreme sports are not necessarily any riskier than more traditional athletic pursuits such as football, hockey, soccer or even running. The key is risk management: wearing protective gear and staying within your comfort zone and skill level.

Ketchum, ranked fourth nationally in women's street skating by the Aggressive Skaters Association, has never broken a bone skating.

"I've probably strained one ligament in my knee, and another time had a pretty deep bruised knee after I lunged too soon and fell on a launch box," she said.

Protecting Yourself Before You Play

In addition to the high skill level she has attained, Ketchum works hard to be so lucky. While she's away at college—Ketchum just finished her sophomore year at the University of Tampa (Fla.)—she works out six days a week, and skates usually every day. Doug McKenney, the Buffalo Sabres' strength and conditioning coach, designed a workout regimen for Ketchum that she follows all year. Weightlifting, aerobic conditioning and flexibility are all part of the package.

"I stretch before I get started; I learned to do that growing up playing soccer," Ketchum said.

Ketchum's in-line path hasn't been all smooth. Every skater learns from experience about wearing cushioning to absorb the usual bumps and bruises. Ketchum always wears a helmet and knee pads when Rollerblading at a skate park.

"When I skate 'street' I don't wear the helmet anymore, but for a beginning skater I'd definitely recommend it," she said.

Knowing Your Limits Reduces Injuries

Perception and reality surrounding "extreme sports" often pedal down different paths. Some school-age kids choose boarding, biking or blading as a refuge from team sports and the pressures attached to them by coaches, parents and classmates. Some practice their tricks to the accompaniment of music that only someone under 30 could love. But choosing the ramp less traveled, or admiring athletes such as Hoffman who push their sport to its utmost extremes, doesn't mean they are reckless thrill seekers. The image of young daredevils trying to fly over "vert" ramps before they've earned their wings is so not happening.

"Some people seem to think that kids on bikes are looking for adrenaline by throwing themselves down stairs and hand rails, but I think I speak for a vast majority of BMXers when I say that's really not true," said Rob Lorenz, a 20-year-old BMX rider from Hamburg. "Nobody wants to get hurt. . . . There's always a chance of injury looming, but no one seeks it out.

"I've had many injuries over the years, the most recent of which was a dislocated shoulder (in December [2003]) and a pretty nasty black eye.

With the exception of snowboarding . . . none of the other so-called "extreme sports" carries a particularly high risk of injury.

"I've also had several broken ankles, sore wrists for life, as well as many various scars on my shins and elbows."

Lorenz says injuries are inevitable for BMXers as they progress to higher levels.

"In any sport, there is a cost to progression," he said, "and although I don't exactly agree that BMX is a 'sport' per se, I will agree that there certainly is a fairly high amount of injuries."

Perceptions Vs. Statistics

Statistically, BMX and its like are not high-risk activities, compared with other sports.

The most useful data available is from the 2002 "Comprehensive Study of Sports Injuries in the U.S.," compiled by American Sports Data in Hartsdale, a suburb outside New York City. The study breaks down the injury rate by sport, which is the number of injuries per 1,000 "athlete exposures," as well as total injuries per sport.

Using injuries per 1,000 exposures, boxing ranks first, with 5.2, followed by tackle football and snowboarding, both at 3.8. Ice hockey is fourth with 3.7, soccer is sixth at 2.4 and softball seventh at 2.2.

"With the exception of snowboarding, which ranks third, none of the other so-called 'extreme sports' carries a particularly high risk of injury," the report says. "Surfing is 10th in risk potential (1.8 injuries), mountain biking 18th, skateboarding 22nd and BMX 24th. In-line roller skating places 27th with only 0.4 injuries per 1,000 athlete exposures."

Similar Numbers Across the Border

The numbers are similar in Canada. The government's Canadian Hospital Injury Reporting Program compiles statistics on sports injuries that were treated in hospitals. Their most recent [as of June 2004] study found that 20 percent of sports injuries treated in hospitals last year were from hockey, followed by: cycling (17 percent), soccer (12 percent), snowboarding (11 percent), basketball (8 percent), baseball, football and in-line skating (7 percent), skiing and skateboarding (5 percent).

Doug Wyseman, a risk management consultant in Woodstock, Ont., who works with municipal governments on skate park planning and liability issues, points out that many sports injuries go unreported or untreated.

"Kids get hurt skateboarding, but it's sort of a badge of honor," he said.

Dr. Guy Brisseau is the chief trauma surgeon at Women and Children's Hospital. He noted that trauma injuries rise in the summer, when children are out of school, but he said it's hard to break down their cases by particular sports.

"We see injuries from biking and skateboarding in the summer, and skiing and snowboarding in the winter," he said.

"We see a fair number of hockey injuries as well. Soccer and baseball—we don't see those as much, but it's difficult to define what an 'extreme' sport is."

Injuries Are a Challenge to Overcome

Injuries do occur, of course. Breaking a bone after falling off a ramp or slamming into a fence will test the resilience of the hardiest biker, blader or boarder. Resilience often wins.

Charlie Crumlish, 17, of Amherst was riding his skateboard outside an Eggertsville school last month. He was "grinding a rail" when he slipped off and came down on his foot. He felt some pain, but he wasn't finished.

Crumlish got back on his skateboard, and back on the rail. He fell off a couple of more times before nailing the trick, and ultimately going for x-rays.

The diagnosis was a small fracture that sidelined him for a few weeks.

"I had ridden down other rails and always nailed them the first time," he explained. "It didn't really hurt that much."

Persisting Despite Injury

Bob Edson, 22, is a skilled BMX rider from Hamburg who rides all over Western New York, from outdoor trails to indoor skate parks. Edson suffered a broken leg back in February [2004] while practicing some of his standard bike moves at an indoor skate park.

"I was riding like normal, and I just landed badly, right on the leg," said Edson, who had a titanium rod inserted in his leg to support the fractured bone.

Edson has been on crutches since and is only now able to gingerly pedal a bit on a mountain bike.

The beginning of summer is a tough time for a cyclist to be unable to practice his hobby, and Edson said his injury will not deter him from returning to BMX.

"It will kind of make me enjoy it even more when I can ride," he said. "It's a really fulfilling thing to do. Now that I can't do it, it's hard to find ways to occupy my time. I wouldn't think of giving it up."

Edson said that to some extent, being a novice is safer than being an advanced cyclist.

Every sport or physical activity carries some level of risk, but the risk of living a sedentary life may be greater.

"If some kid just started riding, he won't be trying the things I'm doing," Edson said. "It's like a building block thing. The majority of people stay at whatever level they're at, without pushing it too much."

Location Makes a Difference

Heidi Lemmon of Los Angeles is the founder of the Skate Parks Association of the USA, a trade association for skate park operators. While it's in her interest to promote the use of skate parks, she says that statistics show they are much safer than skating, boarding or biking on the street.

"Only two kids have died in a skate park since I've been doing this for eight years," Lemmon said by phone from her Los Angeles office. "By comparison, they average nine deaths a year (nationwide) in high school high jumping.

"You see serious injuries with skateboarders when you put them on the street. You put them in a park, the injury rate goes way down."

Laurie Cousins of Olean [New York] likes her three children to skate in parks. Last year, she grew tired of chaperoning them around upstate New York to find parks, so she and her partner, Chris Maynard, decided to open a park of their own.

The park mandates some safety rules—such as everyone wears a helmet—while questions such as when to wear pads are left up to individuals.

"Bones can be fixed; brain damage can't," she said.

SPA USA's Lemmon observed that every sport or physical activity carries some level of risk, but the risk of living a sedentary life may be greater.

"You can sit your kid in front of a TV all day, and they'll develop heart disease and die," she said. "I don't think we want to do that. If your whole focus is to not have injuries, you won't have happy or healthy kids."

2

Dangers of Extreme Sports Can Be Minimized with Proper Safety Techniques

Brad Buxton

Brad Buxton is a writer for Combat Edge, *a publication providing coverage and analysis of military and naval science.*

With extreme sports having a great risk of death and injury, taking proper safety precautions to reduce these risks is essential. Specialized equipment is needed to allow the athlete enough of a safety margin to prepare for accidents. In a 2002 incident, a man who went off-roading in a jeep that did not contain the necessary equipment met a tragic end that might have been prevented.

Extreme sports involve the greater risks of death and injury. Often the best risk control measure is not to participate. However, for those who pursue the adrenalin rush, you can help mitigate the risk by using extreme equipment to gain a margin of safety.

Engineers control risk by designing equipment with a margin of safety. For example, if a hoist is nuclear certified to lift 1,000 lb, it must be able to handle a 3,000-lb. design load. The 2,000-lb margin gives the equipment and operator room to maneuver and ensures a safe lift over time.

The same principle applies to extreme sports. Whether you're jumping from perfectly good airplanes or racing cars,

Brad Buxton, "Extreme Sports," *Combat Edge*, U.S. Department of the Air Force, vol. 12.3, August 2003.

you need extreme equipment to give you an added margin of safety to control your risk.

Off-Roading Trip Turns Tragic

The fatality discussed in this story involved a member who enjoyed the extreme sport of off-road 4-wheeling in his purpose-built Jeep. The story ended in tragedy, in part because the member did not leave himself enough of a safety margin to absorb the unexpected.

On a Friday [during the summer of 2002], the member left work with his supervisor to grab a tow bar so that he and a friend could tow his Jeep south to the beautiful Blanca Peak area near Alamosa, Colorado. They met other friends and camped under the stars that night anticipating a weekend of off-road fun with their 4-wheeling club. The member was known for his jeeping skills and instructed other enthusiasts. That Saturday there were three Jeeps in a convoy working their way up Lake Como Road in Alamosa County. The member had not used his particular Jeep in over 2 years and was excited to see how his new "Ox Lockers" would perform. The positive traction devices would get their test this weekend on some of the most challenging trails in the area.

Jaws 2

At or about 3:00 p.m., the member was making his fourth attempt over a very challenging rock obstacle with a steep grade below it known as "Jaws 2." According to the Colorado State Police, "several people have lost their lives trying to climb the area." The member had been foiled during his first three attempts and even had to straighten his tie-rod after bending it in an earlier attempt.

According to witnesses, the member then decided to attack the Class V (most difficult) challenge on the "high side." The police report states, "He got too close to the right side of 'Jaws 2.'" The Jeep started to tip backward and he gave it more gas which caused it to flip over. The Jeep then started rolling and flipping down off the left side of the trail. It rolled and flipped for 190 feet before it crossed over the trail again and headed another 40 feet down an embankment. The Jeep came to rest on its left side against a large tree. The member did have his lap seat belt on and was not thrown from the vehicle. However, he had a severe head injury and died within about 10 minutes of the crash.

The member's roommate heard the tragic news first. The rest of the unit took the news equally hard.

Whether you're jumping from perfectly good airplanes or racing cars, you need extreme equipment to give you an added margin of safety to control your risk.

From a safety standpoint, the tragedy could have been avoided if the member had not chosen to attempt the climb. This member, like many others, didn't live life backing down from challenges. Thus, the fatal decision to challenge the trail for a fourth time is not what the rest of this article will focus on.

Margin of Safety

Instead, the rest of the article is about margin. The member's equipment was legal for off-road 4-wheeling, but extreme sports require extreme equipment.

First and foremost, the member died from a head injury due to striking a rock. Had the member been wearing a helmet, he may have survived that impact.

Secondly, the member was only wearing a lap belt. Witnesses described seeing his torso being thrown in and out of the protective roll bar cage. Had he been wearing a 5-point harness, he may have stayed within the protection of the roll cage.

Thirdly, the roll bar itself was factory and gave way being torn loose and bent up and forward of the passenger seat. It's hard to say if a stronger roll bar would have offered enough protection, but an aftermarket roll bar could have definitely been more robust.

Finally, his Jeep had been altered since he'd last used it. The "Ox Locker" positive traction device was cited by one friend as the main cause of the accident. Traction and torque were delivered where the normal slippage of the factory differential was expected. Using essentially new equipment to negotiate an obstacle that had taken life before reduced the member's margin of safety below what he needed to live.

In this sad tale, the decision to attempt the climb itself was disastrous, but the four factors just discussed eroded any margin of safety the member needed to survive. If you attempt extreme sports, don't reduce your margin of safety by using low quality safety gear. It's important to remember that you pay for what you get, and what you get may save your life.

3

Extreme Risks of Cliff Jumping Appeal to Thrill-Seekers

Scott Willoughby

Scott Willoughby is a staff writer for the Denver Post.

Despite the risks of BASE jumping, including fines and jail time for participating on National Park land, and a high probability of death, thrill seekers are attracted to the dangers and adrenaline rush that accompany jumps from 300-foot cliffs in Moab, Utah.

Moab, Utah. Three hundred feet. Consider it for a moment. The length of a football field. A chip shot. A long way to fall without a parachute. A short distance to fall with one.

Rest assured that the BASE jumpers launching those 300 feet from the sandstone cliffs of Moab have considered it for more than a moment. The distance is calculated, the risks weighed. The reward is nonpareil.

"There is risk involved, and that's part of the attraction," said Jimmy Pouchert, who, along with his wife, Marta Empinotti, owns and operates Vertigo Base Outfitters in Moab. "High-risk sports allow you to feel so alive. That's why I'm in it. I'm never happier than that brief moment when you leave the cliff and you free-fall before the parachute deploys. For that moment, you forget everything and become so focused. Very few things in life demand 110 percent of your focus and attention like that. It seems like we put so much into those few moments that we get a lot out of it."

A Precise Sport

Unlike the more traditional sky divers, BASE jumpers—considered by many the furthest reach of the extreme sports fringe—hurl themselves from fixed objects such as cliffs and bridges. "BASE" stands for "building, antenna, span and earth." Launch sites, described in "Matrix"-like vernacular as "exit points," therefore tend to be disturbingly close to landing zones. And precision is requisite.

"In Moab, these cliffs are low and you have to be on it," Pouchert said. "You don't have a lot of time to make any decisions, much less the wrong one."

For BASE jumpers the preparation begins long before Pouchert's proclaimed moment of freedom. Hours upon hours of training begin the progression, with a bare bones minimum of 100 sky dives required to learn how to operate the canopy well enough to avoid falling victim to the old sky diving saw: "I've never been hurt jumping before. Only landing."

From there, additional instruction in BASE jumping techniques is required, and perhaps most important, so is an intimacy with your equipment.

"Anyone with serious considerations of this sport takes time to know the gear," said Steve Armstrong, a three-year BASE jumper from Westminster. "I can pack my sky diving canopy in five minutes, but I'll take a half-hour to pack my BASE jumping canopy. It's essentially the same thing, but I'm more thorough with the BASE canopy because it's your only chance of surviving. Three hundred feet is really low."

Risking Fines and Prison

Still, Moab, with a seemingly endless expanse of vertical cliffs between 300 and 400 feet, is among the most popular destinations for BASE jumpers in the West. The same reasoning that drew Pouchert and Empinotti to set up shop beneath the rock walls of Utah's Canyon Country attracted Armstrong and about 75 other adventurers to the rim last Thanksgiving weekend for the annual Turkey Boogie gathering of BASE jumpers. Sure, there are other nearby places to jump. But unlike Moab, few of them are legal.

Jumpers continue to violate the ban somewhat regularly, risking a $2,000 fine, jail time and confiscation of equipment costing up to $3,000 should they get caught.

"This is the best cliff jumping in the United States," Pouchert insists before qualifying his statement. "The best 'legal' cliff jumping in the United States, that is. It's legal to BASE jump on any (Bureau of Land Management) land in the country. It's just that this is one of the few places with vertical cliffs on BLM land. When you get the really tall cliffs, it tends to turn into a National Park. And there's a blanket ban against jumping at any National Park."

Most famous among those illegal National Park jump sites is Yosemite in California, where the prominent, 3,500-foot granite monolith of El Capitan has attracted jumpers since free-fall photographer Carl Boenish led a group to the summit and produced a spectacular short film of their jumps in 1978. The film inspired several jumpers to visit Yosemite Valley, and the National Park Service, not knowing how to react to this new sport, eventually banned it.

But jumpers continue to violate the ban somewhat regularly, risking a $2,000 fine, jail time and confiscation of equipment costing up to $3,000 should they get caught. Perhaps most well-known among the defiant was a group that arranged a 1999 protest against the ban in response to the death of Frank Gambalie III. Gambalie drowned in the Merced River earlier that year while trying to escape from park police after a successful jump off El Capitan.

Death Toll Mounts as Illegal Jumps Continue

Among the half-dozen protesters was experienced BASE jumper Jan Davis of California, who, according to Nick Di Giovanni's *World BASE Fatality List* Web site, became the fifth person to die while BASE jumping in Yosemite Valley. According to accident reports, Davis and the others announced their intentions to park officials and agreed to be arrested after the protest jump, accept a fine and have their equipment confiscated. As a result, Davis used borrowed equipment she was not familiar with, and her canopy never deployed.

Perceptions of the sport are changing as equipment improvements enhance its safety record, Pouchert says, slowly increasing access to exit points. But according to local jumpers, there still are no legal jump sites within Colorado, although the Royal Gorge suspension bridge opens one day a year for qualified jumpers during the annual Go Fast Gorge Games every summer. That's not to say no one is jumping in Colorado however; illicit BASE jumps tend to be kept on the down-low until catastrophe strikes. Two jumping fatalities from the Royal Gorge are listed among the 86 deaths on Di Giovanni's Web site, along with a third from Black Canyon National Park near Delta.

Still, the passion local jumpers feel for this at once intimidating and intoxicating sport willingly keeps them coming back for more.

"We're definitely not normal," Armstrong said. "A lot of sports are similar, but really, nothing in the world can be compared to this."

4

Healing War's Wounds
[Through Extreme Sports]

Karen Breslau

Karen Breslau is the San Francisco Bureau Chief for Newsweek. *She is the author of* Back from the Dead, *and has also been published in the* New York Times Magazine.

As medical treatment for battle wounds improves and more lives are saved, the U.S. military must find new ways to help soldiers with severe injuries cope with a new way life. Extreme sports are one way in which wounded veterans can bridge the gap between the intense physical risks they faced in combat and their return to civilian living.

"Hey, have any of y'all seen the crocodile that got my arm?" U.S. Army Maj. Anthony Smith hoists his prosthetic hook, tied to a paddle, as he floats down Idaho's Salmon River in a large blue raft, manned by a cackling crew of fellow amputees. Momentarily rattled, a group of rafters resting onshore stare as Smith's boat glides by, before someone on the beach points down the rapids and yells, "He went that-a-way." Smith, digging his paddle back into the water, growls with mock pirate glee. "You should see what happens when I'm in a restaurant and I say to the waitress 'Can you give me a hand?'"

He can laugh now. It's the surest sign yet of the progress he's made since April 24, 2004, when Smith, then a captain with an Arkansas National Guard unit stationed near Baghdad, was struck by a rocket-propelled grenade. The three-foot-long missile lodged in his right hip, exploding as Smith's commanding officer rushed to help him. The blast cut Smith's rescuer in half. It blew off Smith's right arm and ripped open his abdomen, destroying one kidney and shredding his intestines, and shattering his femur and right hip. Heat from the explosion burned his retinas and melted his dog tags into his chest. As Smith staggered to his feet, insurgents opened fire, shooting him four times. By the time medics reached him minutes later, Smith had "flat-lined." Finding no pulse or respiration, they loaded him into a body bag and put his name on the list of those KIA, killed in action. Only as a soldier was preparing to zip shut the bag did she notice an air bubble in the blood oozing from Smith's neck wound. "They said, 'Hey, this guy's still alive,'" Smith says.

Two and a half years later, Smith recounts his own resurrection in vivid detail—not because he remembers (he was in a coma for six weeks), but because he has pieced the story together from conversations with his wife, Jackie, and the dozens of doctors who labored to save him. Smith has endured more than 30 surgical procedures to reconstruct his abdomen, the remains of his right arm, his burned face and the gaping wound in his hip, now painfully infected. He must be constantly monitored for signs of traumatic brain injury that may have resulted from the force of his skull's slamming against the inside of his helmet.

Treating All the Scars

Though Smith's tale of survival is extreme, it is no longer unheard of. Thanks to advances in combat medicine and body armor, more than 90 percent of the 20,000 U.S. forces wounded to date [September 2006] in Iraq and Afghanistan are surviving their injuries. (In Vietnam, that figure was closer to 75 percent.) That is encouraging news, to be sure, especially as the U.S. body count in the Iraq war approaches 2,600. But it also presents a huge challenge for the military as this sizable population of wounded veterans returns to society, bearing complex disabilities that will require lifelong care.

To address the problem, the military has adopted a holistic mind-body approach, deploying a fleet of experts ranging from orthopedic surgeons to therapists to work on the wounded. Doctors insist on group therapy to help cope with the guilt that often dogs survivors who have lost—or left— comrades on the battlefield. Of special concern are the service members, like Smith, classified by the Pentagon as "severely injured"—having lost limbs or eyesight, or suffering burns, paralysis or debilitating brain injuries that will not emerge fully in some cases for years. "Technology has advanced to the point where we can salvage patients who would not have survived before," says Lt. Col. John McManus of the Army's Institute for Surgical Research in San Antonio, Texas. "The bigger test is psychological. Can we restore a life worth living?"

Patients who work out regularly, lifting weights and yanking pulleys from their wheelchairs, often with burned and mangled limbs, are rewarded with all-expenses-paid outdoor expeditions.

The Pentagon has recently begun testing more experimental methods, rehabilitating wounded service members with extreme sports designed to build muscle—and self-confidence. Early [in 2007] the Center for the Intrepid, a privately funded $45 million rehab facility featuring rock-climbing walls and an indoor surfing tank, will open on the grounds at Brook Army Medical Center in San Antonio, offering lifelong privileges to those wounded in Iraq and Afghanistan. At BAMC, wounded soldiers are encouraged to get moving as soon as possible, a strategy that promotes independence and wards off depression. Learning to accept their disfigured bodies is "an immense emotional challenge," says Dan Blescini, a psychiatric nurse at BAMC. "They want to know 'Am I a man? Is someone going to love me?' This isn't exactly the stuff you expect the Army to talk about, but this is what's on everyone's mind."

Extreme Sports as Therapy

Patients who work out regularly, lifting weights and yanking pulleys from their wheelchairs, often with burned and mangled limbs, are rewarded with all-expenses-paid outdoor expeditions. It was just such an invitation that brought Smith, two other wounded service members and their wives to the Salmon River last month. They were the guests of Sun Valley Adaptive Sports—one of several private nonprofits consulting with the Pentagon. On the week's agenda: white-water rafting, paragliding, rock climbing and horseback riding. With the group is Erik Schultz, a backcountry sports enthusiast who was paralyzed in a skiing accident eight years ago. During his darkest depression, says Schultz, friends "literally dragged me" on a camping trip. After a week in the wilderness, "I was bursting with self-confidence. Things didn't seem that hard anymore." He hopes that his presence in a wheelchair, fly-fishing from a rocky beach and whooping his way down the river, will help "demystify" disabled life for the wounded service members.

Free from their hospital routines, and the weight of their wounds, Smith and the others spend their days splashing like kids. U.S. Marine S/Sgt. Damion Jacobs, who lost his right leg below the knee to an IED near Fallujah [Iraq] six months ago, removes his prosthetic and props it in the sand like a coffee table; he leans against it while watching the show. Jacobs plans to take his Marine Corps physical and return to active duty. Army Spc. Andrew Soule, an intense, dignified 25-year-old who has emerged as the star of BAMC's rehab program, says that before his injury, he wasn't "much of an athlete." A year ago Soule lost both legs and suffered a severe arm injury in a bomb blast in Afghanistan. Now he kayaks, hand-cycles and surfs. On the first day of the river trip, one of Soule's carbon-fiber prosthetics is fractured. He tosses the limb aside and, for the next five days, kayaks legless, dragging his body over rocky beaches, even climbing stairs, with his arms. "People have this tendency to overreact," says Soule, who left Texas A&M after 9/11 to join the Army. "They don't know how much you can do for yourself." Even Soule is amazed by how far he has come. As he lay tourniqueted on the ground last year next to the wreck-age of his Humvee near the Pakistani border, waiting for a helicopter to rescue him, Soule's squad leader leaned over him and instructed the young soldier to repeat over and over, "I'm going to live. I'm going to live." It's a lesson he carried with him, down the Salmon River and beyond.

5

Delaware School Athletics Incorporate Extreme Sports to Fight Obesity

Alison Kepner

Alison Kepner is a reporter for Delaware Online.

Administrators in Delaware schools are changing the physical education curriculum in schools in an effort to fight the rise of childhood obesity. By changing traditional school athletics to involve more wide-appealing activities, from yoga to skateboarding, administrators hope to encourage students to find physical activities they can pursue into adulthood for a lifelong healthy habit.

Senior Carley Van Sickle has a lot of options for working up a sweat in her Brandywine High School gym class. None requires a rubber ball.

Don't tell "DodgeBall" rivals White Goodman and Peter La Fleur, but physical education teachers across the country are replacing their sport—and kickball and other traditional gym class games—with aerobics, yoga, skateboarding, dance and Ultimate Frisbee.

The idea is to engage children in physical activities they actually may continue as adults. It is another strategy in the battle against America's obesity epidemic.

"Once they get out of high school, they still need to exercise, and they still need to be concerned about healthy nutrition," Brandywine High teacher Sandy Kupchick said.

Alison Kepner, "Gym Classes Knock Out Tradition," *The News Journal/Delaware Online*, February 2, 2007. Reproduced by permission.

Van Sickle, 18, can choose from a dance video game, climbing wall or treadmills. Boxing bags, weight machines and Wave boards—a skateboard adaptation—are other options.

In middle school, "we played a lot of games, nothing like fitness," she said. "This helps you build muscle and tone."

Taking a Different Approach

The "new P.E." slowly is being implemented across Delaware, said John Ray, the state's physical education specialist. "It's about lifetime wellness," he said.

About 65 percent of Americans 20 and older are either overweight or obese, according to the National Health and Nutrition Examination Survey for 1999 to 2002.

The problem begins young and is going younger. About 17 percent of Americans 6 to 19 years old are overweight, triple the figure in the 1970s. The number of overweight children ages 2 to 5 has doubled in the same period, the Centers for Disease Control and Prevention reports.

CDC officials cite research showing most overweight children become obese adults; one study found about 80 percent of those overweight at 10 to 15 years old were obese at 25.

That is why physical education instructors don't want lessons limited to sports. They want students to learn "fitness for life."

Delaware requires physical education classes for elementary and middle school students, but the regulation has no minimum time. The average elementary student spends 30 to 45 minutes per week in phys ed class, Ray said. State officials haven't calculated a middle school average.

The state mandates one credit of physical education for high school students, leading most to take a half-credit class in ninth grade and a second in 10th. Some upperclassmen, such as Van Sickle, opt for an elective class, but many have no physical education after 10th grade.

Skateboarding in Third Period

One of the best physical education programs in the country is located at a school about an hour's drive north of Wilmington. The National Association for Sport and Physical Education twice has recognized Carl Sandburg Middle School in Levittown, Pa., for its classes, which focus on "contemporary lifetime activities."

The school with grades six to nine offers in-line skating, biking, ballroom dancing, orienteering, self-defense, snorkeling, canoeing and kayaking. Students use heart-rate monitors, pedometers and activity monitors, along with digital video replay for movement analysis.

Most of the equipment—from the canoes to the bicycles—was purchased using grant money, which is true in Delaware schools as well. Teachers have been aggressive in their search for financing, looking for nontraditional sources such as fish and wildlife associations.

Basketball and soccer are in the curriculum, too, but "the kids who otherwise normally wouldn't be involved in activity would not be involved if we did all games like that," department chairwoman Terry Martian said.

A free, four-day-a-week intramural program offers students more time to swim, walk on the outdoor trails, work out in the fitness room or play a game in the gym.

Whether it is square dancing or handball, the teachers want students to find an activity they enjoy. "We just hope that it leads to more kids being active, choosing to be active as adults," Martian said.

Student Appeal

At Brandywine High, ninth-graders spend class playing traditional team sports. But they also learn about how fast their hearts should beat during moderate and vigorous exercise. In 10th grade, the curriculum shifts to "lifetime" sports: tennis, golf, aerobics and badminton.

Kupchick experiments with new equipment, always searching for activities that will engage more students. Many quickly took to Wave boards, which have wheels that riders can rotate 360 degrees by twisting their hips and shoulders.

Senior Jonathan Fountain, a skateboarder, said the board isn't only fun but gives him a good workout, too.

"You've got to use your hips," he said, adding it also helps improve balance. "You've got to keep moving, like on a bike."

Senior Danielle Jackson prefers Dance Dance Revolution, a musical meeting of "Simon Says" and "Twister." The popular music video game is played on a mat with four arrow panels: left, right, up and down. Players step on the panels, responding to the screen's arrows, which are synchronized to the song's beat. It is part of the reason she looks forward to physical education class.

"You can do what you want," Jackson said. "You have fun while you are exercising."

Starting Young

The shift from traditional games to fitness-focused activities is evident in elementary schools, too.

North Laurel Elementary School teacher Garrett Lydic knows dodgeball still is played in some state physical education classes "but not in this school."

It turns out, 8-year-olds enjoy Dance Dance Revolution as much as 18-year-olds.

Lydic, Delaware's 2006 Teacher of the Year, wants his students to learn life fitness activities—and not to shy away from physical activities because they always are picked last for a team or feel pressured performing in front of their peers.

"We introduce them to activities that they can do for a lifetime," Lydic said. "We stress quality of life more than anything else."

Lydic grew up playing basketball in school. "The emphasis was on points, and we had a scoreboard in every game that we did," he said. "Now, we don't keep score."

Lydic, who also incorporates spelling and math problems into his lessons, just wants his students to be moving, and knows that they will keep doing so if they are having fun, too.

Getting Kids Excited About Movement

His students enjoy climbing, juggling and scooter activities. They bowl and jump rope. And, it turns out, 8-year-olds enjoy Dance Dance Revolution as much as 18-year-olds.

Lydic teaches skills such as dribbling and shooting, but he incorporates the skills into activities besides the games.

About a week ago, a boy in Lydic's class raised his hand with a question. "He asked if we are ever going to play dodgeball," Lydic said.

He told him, "Not everybody in here likes to be hit by the ball, and not everybody in here feels comfortable with that."

Making sure students have fun and feel comfortable in class is important to Lydic. He emphasizes good sportsmanship.

"All it takes is one bad experience in physical activity or my class to turn someone off" from such activities for life, he said.

"Physical education is really about getting kids excited about movement rather than learning different games and learning how to play different sports," Lydic said.

And that's something that can last a lifetime.

6

Popularity of Extreme Sports May Be a Temporary Fad

Rob Rinehart

Rob Rinehart is an adjunct professor of kinesiology at California State University, San Bernardino. He has published two books on alternative sports and several research articles.

With the increased television X Games viewership and new extreme sports appearing in each winter Olympics, questions about the longevity of alternative sports' popularity are raised. In addition, conflict between the images of "counter-culture" and the "freedom" extreme sports competitors wish to portray, and the growing commercialism imposed on alternative sports by marketing and media continues to mount.

Nobody really knows where it will peak—or even *if* it will end. There are guesses by journalists, by media moguls and corporate seers, by kids swarming like locusts over the urban landscape, gathering on the streets and in the parks and meandering in sanctioned and non-sanctioned areas, by people betting their livelihood on it and by people only marginally interested: when might this media blitz of alternative sports, of wakeboarding, barefoot jumping, sportclimbing, skateboarding, snowboarding, windsurfing, and in-line skating—and more—abate?

Is the cultural formation that is "extreme" sports a fad that will end with the maturation of Gen X, or might it prophesy a

Rob Rinehart, *To The Extreme: Alternative Sports Inside and Out*. Albany: New York Press, 2003. Copyright © 2003 State University of New York. All rights reserved. Reproduced by permission of the State University of New York Press.

paradigmatic shift in how western societies view sport? Will a new sport ethic gradually supersede the current highly competitive one? Does extreme sport foretell a global sport ethic, or is it a Westernized phenomenon, pretty much confined to English-speaking, colonized sport culture? Does performing the sports—that is, the actual activities themselves—drive the *need* for the sports, or might this relatively new, alternative sport culture scape be driven by a cynical, mass-produced, media-oriented, economically-based cultural blitz that must have new and younger consumers in order to survive? Are there significant differences among the new extreme sports, or do the sports follow similar patterns of status—emerging, resisted, grudgingly accepted, mainstreamed (or dominant), passé, obsolete—and are they merely at different stages of very similar processes? Can we look at these sports as creating effects upon culture and in turn being created by cultural effects as profoundly as other cultural formations and artifacts have? Such cultural formations might include media, multinational corporations, or political/ideological movements. Obviously, alternative sports are interwoven with other cultural formations; any attempts to sort out the threads of each result in a less-than-accurate view of the alternative sportscape.

These questions are important ones, and I can only hope to touch on them, primarily through the case of in-line skating. The questions assume a complex 'constellation' of interrelationships, which I may only hope to better expose through discussion. As Walter Benjamin is said to have written to Theodore Adorno, "The great book of the future . . . will consist of fragments torn from the body of other work; it is a reassembly, a patchwork quilt of meanings already accomplished."

A Change in Perception

Though sports icons still are relegated to types, the generalized mythos of the westernized, Americanized 'hero' has lost a bit of allure, a bit of credibility, so that 'general truths'—in this case, stereotypes—slightly miss the mark for most consumers, and are thus replaced by more specific stories which reflect actual lived circumstances. Our heroes have been shown to be fallible. Indeed, the dynamic, mediated process between positive icon-making and negative destruction of the icon was standard procedure in the 1990s: from the capitalistically driven multinational media, both good and bad examples make for good 'stories.'

This is not to say that cultural tropes have ceased to exist (at least in the public's imagination), but rather that the assumed homogeneity and totalization of audience is no longer a credible assumption, though an increasingly homogeneous media attempts to portray totalized audiences.

Ironically, athletes may be giving up that part of themselves that they most sought to find through alternative sports: their freedom.

The trickle-down effect of these mainstream-sport strategies upon more marginalized sports like in-line skating encourages athletes who want to remain viable in their sport to create their own marketing personality. Also, it encourages the very wealthy to hire agencies to help them with their commercial image. Within extreme sports, projected incomes make this very feasible for the top tier of recognizable sports stars.

For more individual sports (such as extreme sports as opposed to team sports like NBA basketball), the strategy may be a good one, albeit decidedly calculated. The problems of this 'cult of personality'—or icon-making process—may be that the athletes literally give up their own 'agency' when they sign with agents, or when they sign with corporations. This, of course, may be antithetical to the claimed ideologies—like freedom, individuality, and an ethos proclaiming an aesthetic lifestyle—for many extreme sports and sport extremists.

Athletes occasionally emulate, without the strong ideological and historical backdrop of 'sanctified' sport (that is, mainstream sport—whose legitimacy is rarely questioned), professional wrestlers in their hucksterism. Thus, they risk destroying the credibility that they may have spent much of their young adult lives fostering. As in sports television strategies, the athlete's personality becomes constructed, with shrewd aims at marketing strategies, for the least common denominator: that is, the largest market. And, ironically, athletes may be giving up that part of themselves that they most sought to find through alternative sports: their freedom.

Mainstream athletes—pros—see their sport primarily as work; alternative sport professionals still insist their sport is part of their lifestyle, thus still 'fun.'

Still, the processes of icon-making and commodification are interdependent. In fact, many of the athletes *seek* to become commodities, finding lucrative careers through the process. This process is not unlike a symbiotic relationship, where companies, consumers, and individual athletes alike share (but not equally) in the profits. Many of the athletes, in fact, represent smaller corporations: for example, Arlo Eisenberg started Senate, and Angie Walton publishes *Daily Bread*. Consumers do get something from these relationships, not the least of which is a shared lifestyle with famous athletes (status), a use of product (identity), and cultural capital. But the consumer-athlete nexus is a constructed one, one in which both athlete and corporate strategies conspire to create a market of celebrity. . . .

The Price of Commercialism

As professional skaters find themselves involved more and more in doing the sidelight activities that help their careers, they find that they have less time to skate. This effect, not uncommon to successful mainstream athletes, might be termed the "book tour effect." Super Bowl, World Series, Stanley Cup, and NBA Championship winners annually bemoan this effect; however, in this regard, there is at least one major difference between mainstream and extreme sport: the perceived and real degree of 'play' versus 'work' to which athletes might admit. Mainstream athletes—pros—see their sport primarily as their work; alternative sport professionals still insist their sport is part of their lifestyle, thus still 'fun.' Thus, in-liners might see that doing promotions for their sport, being involved in the culture surrounding in-line skating—all of the trappings of the sport—are considered extensions of the in-line lifestyle. . . .

But the skating culture—indeed, the 'extreme' phenomenon—as they once knew it is also morphing, changing to fit the demand of a seemingly voracious television audience. Because of this perception, liquor company Heublein dropped sponsorship of the beach volleyball tour in favor of a more cutting-edge, multiple-event amalgam called the Cuervo Gold Board-to-Board Challenge, which combines snowboarding and wakeboarding. Corporate spokesperson Scott Mueller says, "These events [pro beach volleyball] don't deliver the same message anymore. Alternative sports do, and that's where many of our consumers are now." He might have added that future consumers, in the under-age population, are the potential market for Heublein as well. Thus, Heublein's sponsorship on extreme sports serves a double purpose: it educates the young in consumer behaviors regarding both alcohol use and extreme sport.

What is televised for in-line skating has changed, too. In the first X Games (in 1995), for example, distance (10K) in-line skaters were asked by ESPN to run a downhill race, at that time termed a "once-a-year carnival act for a TV event." Since 1995, the views on whether the in-line downhill is appropriate or too dangerous have changed somewhat: Marvin

Percival, of speed-skating company Sk8Deal (Andover, Massachusetts), recently explained that his own son is interested in what Percival calls the "extremely dangerous" downhill course. Coming from a speed-skating (as opposed to aggressive-skating) background, he says, gives the skaters and the company a "tremendous amount of credibility." This, of course, translates into a greater acceptance of formerly inappropriate kinds of events like the massed downhill. (Thus are sporting events, over time, naturalized as normative.)

What of the larger corporations supporting in-line skating? What are some of their strategies for success? I e-mailed Roces, an Italian-based extreme in-line skating manufacturer, and the firm's International Team Manager Francesco Mattioli responded to my queries. He claims that the skating itself is what promotes the sport best: "It is always amazing to watch aggressive skaters pulling out incredible tricks on vert ramps or in the street. That is what most of our target [audience] likes and wants to see." Furthermore, "every single skater has [his/her] own character and personality and fits perfectly inside the [aggressive] team." Mattioli is, of course, speaking of professionals who are spokespersons for Roces and who skate using Roces gear. This strategy—of a 'cult of personality' for Roces' team members—is quite lucrative: the professionals' "image . . . can sell millions of dollars of products."

But the distinction between 'counterculture' and resistant to more mainstream is quickly eroding. Often the personal strategies of in-liners—utilized so that athletes may remain involved in the sport and marry their passion for in-line with their need for income—also reflect a more global strategy. Skaters believe that their sport is in its infancy and that they must involve themselves in the direction it may take. Control over the sport is important to these athletes, yet it sometimes is in opposition to corporate aims.

Distinguishing Between Media

Clearly, the impact of electronic media is quite different from that of the written media (newspapers, magazines, 'zines). The goals of the two are not necessarily similar, either. While television and video are visual, the written media retell stories, presumably rely on more in-depth coverage, demonstrate a more multivocal array of stances, and find different angles to reanalyze what television has provided sensorily and with immediacy.

For the most part, the images—of products, and now athletes as products or representations of brands—are media imaginings, images that have become almost caricatures of the athletes themselves.

Weaver discusses the standard news story, both on TV and in the newspaper. He writes of a paradox of sorts: the television news broadcast presents "a unified whole," a thematic block produced for easy digestion, whereas the newspaper is made up of "a diverse, numerous, often inchoate aggregate." Newspapers are multivocal; television demonstrates a univocal point of view. Despite this, Weaver claims that television's "stories" are more in-depth and experiential: television reportage

is more analytical, which more consistently and insistently goes beneath and beyond the surface of events to exhibit the larger trends and meanings of current affairs, which achieves the more integrated and coherent exposition of the reporter's findings, and which constitutes the more flexible and sophisticated reportorial instrumentality.

This depth is, of course, largely from an attempted singular point of view.

While he writes about the differences between television and newspaper reportage (and emotional involvement of the "viewer"), Weaver does not, however, discuss affective difference between magazine (whose temporal lag from the moment of 'news' is much greater than that of both TV and newspapers) and television reportage. And Weaver reduces the discussion to unified audience stances. However, a unified audience stance is a fiction.

There are other differences, differences in strategies of the media: for example, the 'hero-making' machines of both types of media are qualitatively different. Skaters are aware of this strategy for co-optation: *In-Line: The Skate Magazine* discussed the electronic media in a cover story titled "espn's extreme games baits the hook with cash and credibility: the hero machine."

However, Arlo Eisenberg says, "The hero you need for ESPN is different than the hero for *Big Brother* [a skating magazine published by Larry Flynt]. Most people can identify with all the heroes on ESPN. In the magazines, they still are [distinguishable] personalities." In other words, on television, the icons/heroes have taken on generalizable, more mainstream, status; in the magazines, they are more niche types.

Media Strategy for Promotion

How does this difference possibly reflect any kind of reality? In many ways, it doesn't (while simultaneously creating new realities and new approaches to old realities). For the most part, the images—of products, and now athletes as products or representations of brands—are media imaginings, images that have become almost caricatures of the athletes themselves. Still, they are viable and profitable methods of gaining audience—and selling product.

For television, whose raison d'être is to reach the largest number of potential buyers possible, privileging the dominant, usually nonoffensive sides of athletes is a solid strategy. Television's use of mainstream ideologies, with occasional "reality-enforcing" oppositions, attempts to position athletes as authentic while simultaneously accessible to a wider variety of audiences. This can be a difficult and tenuous proposition, yet, with the prior knowledge (and expectations) of the sports-television-viewing public, the amalgam of styles can be accomplished. Of course, the overall effect of a given broadcast—or a series of broadcasts—is what becomes mainstream. The totality of ESPN's *X Games* promotes an ideology of kids out having a good time, doing incredibly athletic moves on fairly new implements (in-line skates), and making their way through adolescence in a societally benign manner. Individual skaters may be deemed "bad boys," or "outsiders," but of course that is a requisite stance for mainstream America: the underdog, the misunderstood teenager, the (usually male) kid who is trying to rise above 'his' anger. So, again, this 'type' is relegated into a larger 'multifaceted society' that is presumably reflected in the *X Games'* broadcasts.

The strategy follows one the NBA and Nike and Reebok have used for years: show different 'personalities' of players to create fan identification with a pantheon of stars as reflected in a variety of lines (shoes being the easy example): David Robinson ("clean-cut All American US Naval Academy"), Michael Jordan ("the greatest basketball player ever"), Charles Barkley ("outspoken, honest to a fault, brash"), Dennis Rodman ("odd, hard-working role player who is always in trouble with authority but has a heart of gold"), and so on. But overall, the NBA and the shoe companies have submitted for consumer approval a picture supposedly reflective of American diversity and even, presumably, of tolerance for difference.

In-line skating has followed that strategy, though not so successfully, both globally (on ESPN and Fox Sports) and locally, within the 'subculture' of skating, and in the 'zines. In the skating magazines, the continual education of consumers is fundamental to their identification with any individual skaters. So, magazines have spent a lot of time establishing stars and potential icons. The profile is a staple of each month's issue. Magazines are currently—of course, informally—in the process of establishing rough hierarchies of these stars. And, as in mainstream sport, enthusiasts will claim that the hierarchies are solely based on the tricks each person can perform— but of course in establishing heroes in the magazines, personality, attitude, and style all matter a great deal. Out on the street, performance and bravura matter more, but in the magazines, words reflecting mores are critical. Presentation of self in interviews establishes hierarchies. But a few stars have already become in-line role-niche icons: the ever-present Arlo Eisenberg ("one of the pioneers of skating"), the successful teenager Aaron Feinberg ("won the X Games on his sixteenth birthday—and bought a car"), and women's skater Angie Walton ("an entrepreneur who publishes *Daily Bread*").

Women skaters, not surprisingly but sadly, are not in great demand from corporate sponsors or from the media. But, more distinct personality types—both men and women, boys and girls—are beginning to emerge as ways to establish identities for the skaters with which the consuming public may identify. . . .

The relationships of buyers to brands, and the affinity consumers have for the brands, have superseded thoughtful product choice, and have, in some cases, overcome the ethos that brought consumers to the product in the first place.

Sending a Message

ESPN's images of extreme sports (via the vehicle of the *X Games*) have gained cultural cachet and produced relatively homogeneous and dominant messages of what extreme sports constitute and how extreme sports (and their participants) may behave. But more specifically, the relatively less-established persona of in-line make it an easier target for co-optation than other sports: "ESPN can come along and make

Rollerblading what they want; they can't damage skateboarding." And ESPN, while creating a singular and unified image of extreme sports as competitive, risky, and accessible, have also heavily influenced the image of in-line skating. This serves as an effective co-optation of the sport by a relatively univocal source.

George Trow explains how television has infantilized (and socialized) young people, creating a need, an ache, to become "adult" consumers. He writes, "'adulthood' has been defined as 'a position of control in the world of childhood,'" that adults are behaviorally just older children. Furthermore, the *appearance* of choice—of product choice, of freedom of expression—is seductive, thus problematic: "The permission given by television is permission to make tiny choices, within the context of total permission infected with a sense of no permission at all." Within the medium of cable and network television, ESPN has served as the single most important agency that provides models for the alternative-sport audience, and yet, the nearly singular image that ESPN is providing, and the active disregard for the noncompetitive ethos of alternative sports in general and in-line in particular, provides for Trow's "tiny choices," of choices without any real choice.

But it is part of a larger sports-oriented marketing drive in the late twentieth century and the early twenty-first. Marketers have eschewed the former approach of sponsorship—"because a CEO or CFO 'had a great affinity for the sport'"—in favor of a "brand-development approach" which Nike, Benetton, Roces, and Disney have all utilized successfully. Rather than the CEO being loyal to the sport (and by extension, the fans sharing in that loyalty—with nostalgia toward teams and individuals), the consumers are expected to become loyal to brands that cut across a variety of sportspeople. The brands themselves have become emblematic of the human contact with the sport. And the relationships of buyers to brands, and the affinity consumers have for the brands, have superseded thoughthful product choice, and have, in some cases, over-come the ethos that brought consumers to the product in the first place. . . .

Selling Out

At the inception of the X Games, when no one knew if this extravaganza was going to be a success or not, reports from skaters were more critical of ESPN's handling of in-line. Some of the complaints included: not enough television exposure for women skaters ("If we had worn skimpy clothes, something a little sexier . . . would we have been televised? Probably."), little activity provided for younger skaters after hours, change in formats ("There was no time to recuperate and get your nerve up again," said Jondon Trevena, and there was a double-elimination format, previously unheard of in in-line), addition of an event (the downhill), deletion of an event (a distance 20K), pressures from television schedules which made time a constraining factor, and too large a street final course, to name a few. Shura McComb, a skater who was head judge at the 1995 X Games, summed up the philosophical and lifestyle difference between the skaters and ESPN this way:

> The skaters had fun, but I don't think ESPN had a grasp on in-line skating. They didn't show any sympathy toward what the skaters believe in and didn't have much faith in us as professionals.

In 1999, just four years later, many of the younger skaters were not talking so much about "fun" or about "what the skaters believe in": their concerns were more mainstream, more capitalistic. Younger skaters still write in to skating magazines asking how they might capture corporate sponsorship. One recent letter to the editor in *Daily Bread* engaged in this debate by listing reasons "Why I love being an un-sponsored rollerblader from Mt. Sinai, N.Y." . . .

Why is the fact that ESPN (along with the rest of Disney) serves as a monopoly over athlete image and icon-making a problem? Isn't sport—and entertainment—production a relatively benign entity when compared to, say, tobacco and gun manufacturing? As Benjamin Barber discusses it, the problem is not in capitalism itself. Nor is the problem in consumerism, or in those who would limit consumerism (as he calls it, the dynamic and dialectic between Jihad and McWorld). The problem with Disney cornering the American and international market for something as seemingly benign as alternative sports might be put this way, as Barber states it:

> The problem with Disney and McDonald's is not aesthetics, and the critics of mass taste such as Horkheimer and Adorno (and me) are concerned not to interfere with the expression of private taste, but to prevent monopoly control over information, and to interdict that quiet, comfortable coercion through which television, advertising, and entertainment can constrict real liberty of choice.

When one enters into watching television sport—any kind of televised sport—one has already allowed those agents—the network executives, the directors who decide on what one will see and which angle one will view it from, the marketing firms and agencies and arms of the networks who determine what products will sell with which programming, and the commentators whose oftentimes prewritten scripts fight hard to reinforce the sponsors message—to "constrict real liberty of choice." This is one of the problems with previously resistive sport forms' "stars" seeking to become more and more cultural icons. They became celebrated because they represented, in a real sense, the outer limits of choice; but, having been swallowed whole into the mainstream culture, their presence is even more pathological than if they were clearly mainstream. They demonstrate the punishment that an individual may suffer if she/he chooses to remain individual.

7

Extreme Sports Hype Is Commercialism

Josie Appleton

Josie Appleton writes for several British publications, including Spiked, Times Literary Supplement, The Times (London), and Spectator. She is the author of Museums for the People *and co-inventor of the Manifesto Club.*

Extreme sports are commercialized by an industry eager to make money off new recreational activities. Dangers of extreme sports are often over-exaggerated, and the hype of the benefits that come from trying these new sports overshadows the real potential they offer for personal achievement and satisfaction.

There is a new extreme sport born almost every week, each seemingly more bizarre and dangerous than the last. BASE-jumping involves parachuting off buildings and cliffs; extreme ironing (inexplicably) involves ironing mid-skydive, up a mountain or under water. Hang-gliding and skydiving have spawned helibungee and sky-flying; skateboarding has spawned street luge, or lying on a skateboard and going fast downhill. Buildering is free climbing up skyscrapers, popularised by the Frenchman Alain 'Spiderman' Robert; free running treats the city as one big gymnastics circuit. Then there are events such as the Verbier Extreme, which challenges snowboarders to find the most daring way of descending a mountain.

Extreme sports—also known as lifestyle sports—have roots in 1960s countercultural movements, and have been growing

Josie Appleton, "What's So Extreme About Extreme Sports?" *Spiked*, August 30, 2005.

since the late 1980s. Research by American Sports Data found that new-style sports such as snowboarding and paintballing have increased at the expense of traditional sports. Snowboarding was up by 30 per cent between 1998 and 2004 (7.1 million people tried it at least once in 2004), while paintballing increased by 63 per cent in the same period (to 9.6 million participants), and artificial wall climbing was up by 63 per cent (to 7.7 million). By contrast, the number of baseball players fell by 28 per cent between 1987 and 2000, declining to 10.9 million players (though most of these would be regular players, whereas most paintballers would be one-offs). Softball and volleyball fell by 37 per cent and 36 per cent in the same period.

Given the high-adrenaline image, it's unsurprising that male 15- to 24-year-olds are the prime market. In the UK, Mintel found that 22.7 per cent of 11- to 19-year-olds participated in BMX/mountain biking and 27.5 per cent did skateboarding. But these sports attract a wide variety of participants. BASE jumpers include thirty- and forty-something solicitors and accountants; and the new free running training academy in east London attracts 80 people a session, including everybody from kids to the middle aged.

The Myth of 'Extreme' Sports

But it isn't really the danger factor that marks out extreme sports. According to Nicholas Heyworth from Sports England, many are less dangerous than traditional sports: 'Statistically, the most dangerous sport is horse riding.' One 'aggressive skating' website warns you to 'Skate safe, because pain and death suck!', and another cliff jumping website is packed with disclaimers and warnings, such as 'don't drink and jump', 'never jump alone' and 'know your limits'. Heyworth notes that 'many extreme sports guys have got safety equipment up to their eyeballs, and a complete safety team. You would be lucky to get a cold sponge and a bucket of water at a Sunday league rugby match'. A helicopter packed with medical equipment tracks participants in the Verbier Extreme.

Extreme sport goods—including TV programmes, graffiti art, design, drinks, and clothing—are a bigger business than the sports themselves.

Improvements in equipment allow the reduction in risk and pain. In the 1960s, skydiving was done by penniless daredevils using surplus US airforce chutes. One veteran recalls: 'It hurt like hell and you drifted mercilessly at the will of the wind until you crashed to the ground and it hurt like hell again.' Now, he says, there are 'high-income jumpers who not only make eight jumps a day, but pay someone to pack their parachutes'. Even the most extreme of extreme sports pale [by] comparison beside the exploits of the early climbers and explorers, for whom the risks were great and the outcomes unknown. The advert for Sir Ernest Shackleton's 1914–17 Trans-Antarctic expedition read: 'Men wanted: For hazardous journey. Small wages, bitter cold, long months of complete darkness, constant danger, safe return doubtful. Honour and recognition in case of success.'

Much of the hype about extreme sports comes not from the participants, but from the industry that surrounds it. Extreme sport goods—including TV programmes, graffiti art, design, drinks, and clothing—are a bigger business than the sports themselves. The Extreme Sports Channel has an estimated audience of 20 million across Europe, most of whom wouldn't go anywhere near a half-pipe—it's popular among Portuguese women, for example.

The Extreme Media Group sells a range of clothing and drinks. The 'Extreme energy' drink is formulated to 'deliver an intense physical and mental energy boost', using Asian fermented tea, Siberian ginseng and guarana (a natural form of caffeine). There is even 'Extreme water' ('the pure artesian mineral water from the Rockhead source in Buxton, will rehydrate you fast'), and Extreme Chillout ('new gen soft drink created to aid relaxation, recovery and all round chilling'). Meanwhile, there is an X-Games brand of mobile phone: 'Carry the excitement and attitude of X Games with you everyday. The tweaked out phone allows devoted fans to capture the signature style and personality of the X Games in a wireless phone.'

But it's not all image. Beneath the hype, lifestyle sports are a new kind of sport for a new age. While traditional sports elevated the values of commitment and fair play, these new sports offer individuals a more personal kind of challenge.

From Teamwork to Individual Achievement

Most traditional sports were institutionalised in the final decades of the nineteenth century. Prior to that, sport had been more informal, with the different teams in a rugby match deciding on the rules at the start of the game. Indeed, many sports were just a more or less organised form of fighting: early 'football' involved neighbouring villages scrapping over a pig's bladder.

Now that class and community identity is on the wane, traditional sporting associations have suffered. A boys' football team, for example, requires parents as volunteer helpers, and for each member of the team to play by the rules and turn up for practice. Professor Neil Ravenscroft, a research fellow at the University of Brighton, tells me that 'Volunteers to run sport outside of school are declining. And young people have less commitment to the idea that you adhere to sets of rules that are not yours, and turn up to training regularly'.

Lifestyle sports provide more individualised ways of pushing yourself. There is no winning and losing as such, and little organisation into teams or leagues. Each individual is really competing against himself: the founder of free running, Sebastien Foucan, said that the sport was about a 'desire to overtake yourself'.

Once boys were sent out to freezing football and rugby fields to make men of them; now they might assault a half-pipe instead.

How a free runner tackles the urban landscape is up to him. There are some established moves—a cat jump, speed vault, a palm spin, and so on—but you are always free to invent your own. This contrasts with sports such as gymnastics, when athletes have a certain time to perform, a set piece of equipment and a limited series of moves.

Extreme Sports as a Means of Confrontation

Extreme sports claim to be confronting authority. Rather than work within leagues and sporting bodies, participants say that they are doing it for themselves. Bandit canoeing goes down forbidden waterways, and off-piste snowboarding and skateboarding crash off set tracks. Free runners claim to challenge the official architecture of the city. Ez, who runs the east London free running academy, says: 'I like the freedom aspect, the fact that every individual has their own way of overcoming. The average person will be guided by pavements, but with parkour you interact with obstacles, you won't be guided by them.'

The only rules are those tacitly agreed by participants. A street basketball site or skateboarding half pipe will have a set of agreements about what's allowed. At Brighton skateboarding park, for example, there are different times of the day for different abilities.

For some, lifestyle sports can be character developing. Once boys were sent out to freezing football and rugby fields to make men of them; now they might assault a half-pipe instead. They go at a jump again and again, falling off and picking themselves up until they can finally do it. In this way, you bear the consequences of your actions. One climber explained the attraction: 'there must be something which can be won and something which can be lost. The winning can be the unutterable joy as your questing fingers latch a crucial edge. The losing can be life itself. Either way we choose.'

Extreme sports can also enable you to confront fears. Some free runners are scared of heights, yet will perform complicated leaps between high buildings. They still their minds before the jump, overcome the part of them that wants to balk. This isn't about taking risks for the sake of it: instead, it's the calculated judgement of the sportsman. Ez argues that free running 'requires discipline to do it properly, which is transferred to other aspects of life'. Some claim that the thrill of the jump can cast the grind of everyday life into perspective. One young BASE-jumper says: 'It's the way to refresh things, to keep the mind awake. You have plenty of time to think about yourself, the mountain you stand on, your life, people you meet, things you're doing.'

Of course, some people look to these new sports for easy thrills. They want the appearance of doing something 'craaazy' like skydiving or bungee jumping, while relying on the instructor to ensure that nothing goes wrong. But some participants want to put themselves to the test. This comes at a time when institutionalised sports are being tied up in regulation, with risk analysis required before every rugby game and players suing the referee if they get injured. In schools, kids are encouraged to go for non-cooperative games that reinforce everybody's self-esteem. Lifestyle sports might provide an opportunity for some individuals to develop themselves.

The Limits of Extreme Sports

Because lifestyle sports are so individualised, however, they are liable to go off in bizarre directions. Without social sanction and discipline, these sports can look like the more ridiculous parts of the *Guinness Book of Records*, with people riding bikes up trees or ironing up mountains. This is casting around, looking for something—anything—to test yourself.

These sports can also revel in individuals' isolation, the fact that they don't have to rely on anybody else. This is a limited form of subjectivity: in reality, we develop ourselves by working with and against others. Traditional sports provided a way for individuals to push themselves through the challenge of competition, or by working together as a team. A hundred-metre runner, for example, is trying to beat the other runners rather than just his PB [Personal Best]—and this challenge takes him to new heights. Lifestyle sports can encourage a narcissistic focus on individual performance, rather than pushing the limits of human achievement.

This is why extreme sports are so hyped up: the adrenaline factor is sold in concentrated form.

There is something childish, too, about the desire to traverse official boundaries. Canoeing where you aren't supposed to be canoeing, jumping where you're not supposed to jump . . . this involves the guilty freedom of a child breaking the rules. Paradoxically, an obsession with breaking rules actually leaves you beholden to them.

Moving Past the Hype to Face the Challenge

So there is both potential and limits to extreme sports. In order to understand the pros and cons, though, we have to cut through the hype that surrounds them. This hype owes less to the participants than to the extreme sports industry.

This industry makes the idea of 'living on the edge' into a consumer product. Deep down, we all feel that we should be pushing ourselves a bit more; the extreme sports industry sells the image of aspiration. Wear a 'Just do it' cap; drink a can of

'Live life to the max' Pepsi; talk on an X-Games mobile phone. This is about the appearance of living on the edge, posing at taking risks while actually doing nothing at all. In the passive act of buying a consumer good, you are offered thrills and spills. It's not the real act of grappling with a challenge, but the image of 'pushing it to the MAX'. This is why extreme sports are so hyped up: the adrenaline factor is sold in concentrated form.

Some of these new sports are little more than PR products. There are actually a tiny number of dedicated free-runners, and many will only perform for the camera. The sport became a media phenomenon before it built up a decent base of participants; now it can be more for show than self-development. Extreme sports often have a short shelf life: they will be the in thing for a few months, but soon get overtaken by the next fad. XFL, an 'extreme' version of American football that was a mix of NFL and WWF wrestling, was set up in 2000, but folded after just one season.

So let's put aside the extreme hype, and look at these sports as just another kind of sport. They offer some potential for individual development—although often only by leaping in odd directions.

8

Olympics Continue to Add New Extreme Sports to Lineup

Matt Higgins

Matt Higgins is a reporter for the New York Times.

With each Winter Olympics, extreme sports gain a stronger presence in the world's greatest athletic competition. Skiercross will be added to the 2010 Vancouver Games lineup. An aggressive sport often involving physical contact between competitors and known for some spectacular crashes and serious injuries, skiercross already holds a wide fan base from its appearance in the X Games and looks to gain more enthusiasts upon its Olympic debut.

Added to the Winter X Games 10 years ago as an appeal to youth, skiercross has instead come to be dominated by retired Alpine racers creating a second act to their competitive careers.

A new event for the 2010 Olympic Winter Games in Vancouver, skiercross features four or more racers on a downhill course of big jumps, banks and rollers. Often compared to motocross, competitors bump and jostle one another, leading to some spectacular crashes.

At the X Games on [Jan. 28, 2007], the sport lived up to its reputation for contact on Buttermilk Mountain's 3,600-foot course. Nine of 24 racers fell—three were treated at a hospital and released—beginning with elimination rounds and carrying into a thrilling final. In that race, the Aspen skier Casey Puckett grabbed the lead out of the gate and hung on to win despite a late charge by Jake Fiala of Frisco, Colo.

An Unpredictable Sport

Coming off the course's last jump, where the snowboardcross racer Lindsey Jacobellis wiped out a day earlier, Fiala made a final push to finish first, but he got his tips up while airborne and went skidding to the snow. His momentum carried him across the finish line, and he wound up with the silver medal.

"I knew if I went too far to the left, I wouldn't make the landing," said Fiala, 31, who competed in Alpine events at the 2002 Olympics. "I pretty much flew into the fence."

Puckett, 34, who competed in downhill events at four Olympics from 1992 through 2002, said of Fiala's late push, "I don't want to put people into the fence, but I'm going to protect my lead."

Skiercross will be the third X Games event to be added to the Olympics, joining snowboarding halfpipe and snowboardcross.

Enak Gavaggio, 30, of France finished third, his seventh bronze medal at the Winter X Games. All three women's medalists were French: Ophelie David (gold), Valentine Scuotto (silver) and Meryll Boulangeat (bronze).

The most successful and famous racer in the field was the 33-year-old Daron Rahlves, of Sugarbowl, Calif., who has 28 Alpine World Cup podium appearances in downhill and super-G, including 12 victories. Rahlves retired from Alpine competition after the 2006 Olympics, his third.

Although it was his first Winter X Games, Rahlves was favored to win the gold medal in skiercross after finishing first in qualifying and in each of his quarterfinal and semifinal heats.

But during the final, Rahlves inexplicably lost his balance on an upper portion of the course and went careering sideways off a jump, crashing and losing a ski.

His spill demonstrated how unpredictable skiercross can be.

"The big thing is," Puckett said, "you can be the fastest skier in the world, which Daron arguably is, and still not win the skiercross."

Gaining Momentum

Its simplicity and unpredictability led Ron Semiao, the senior vice president of ESPN Original Entertainment and X Games creator, to add the event for the Winter X Games's second season. No skiing events were held during the first Winter X Games in 1997 because the sport was viewed as stale and stodgy compared with snowboarding.

Since its debut at the X Games, skiercross has become a World Cup discipline governed by the International Ski Federation.

But the sport's biggest boost was its inclusion in the next Winter Olympics. Skiercross will be the third X Games event to be added to the Olympics, joining snowboarding halfpipe and snowboardcross.

With the biggest, most stylish 1080-degree spins, Steve Fischer wound back the clock during the men's superpipe [at the 2007 X Games], winning the gold medal.

Fischer, 24, of Breckenridge, Colo., last won X Games gold in 2004 when he was among a select group of riders who pioneered the 1080, a spin of three full rotations. He has since struggled, finishing out of the top 10 at the X Games, and failing to qualify for the 2006 Olympic team.

But in the X Games final, Fischer beat out three American Olympians, including the halfpipe gold medal winner at the Turin Games, Shaun White, who wound up with silver.

"It's nice to be on top," Fischer said. "This one is great."

Adding Trick Moves

The first of Fischer's three runs turned out to be the winner, with a score of 92. White was second with a 91, and 19-year-old Mason Aguirre of Duluth, Minn., won the bronze with a 90.66.

Since Fischer helped introduce the 1080 three years ago, it has become a requirement for a winning run. All three medal winners included at least two during their routines.

As it turned out, an easier trick undid White.

Because White, 20, of Carlsbad, Calif., finished first in qualifying, he had the last run and a chance to unseat Fischer for gold. He could do no worse than second, but on his final run he landed low on a 540-degree spin known as a McTwist, a relatively midlevel move. On his prior run, White's board struck the deck during a McTwist.

"I had a sketch, and that's what cost me gold," said White, who has not competed in a halfpipe contest since winning the U.S. Open of Snowboarding in March 2006. White has been inundated with commercial opportunities since winning Olympic gold, and he said they have interfered with his riding.

9

Extreme Sports Provide Opportunity for Mentoring

Lauren MacIntyre

Lauren MacIntyre is a writer for New Yorker Magazine.

In Los Angeles and New York, a program called "Stoked" pro-vides an opportunity for inner-city children to learn snowboard-ing and surfing. They are paired with a young professional who mentors and encourages them to become involved in community service and continue their education, rather than turn to drugs and/or gangs to fill their time.

Sachia, a reedy fifteen-year-old from the Lower East Side, is a man of many passions: Nike Air Jordans, limited-edition baseball hats, snowboarding. Until recently, learning to surf was decidedly not among them ("I like hot water, not cold," he said), but to hold his place in the extreme-sports mentor-ing program, Stoked, which, come January, will host the same snowboarding excursions he loved earlier this year, he con-sented to try the wetter sport of wave riding.

Stoked, which has programs in New York and Los Angeles, pairs mentees selected from inner-city schools with young professionals, all of whom are board-sport novices. The eleven pairs in this year's New York surf clinic, the program's second, took five trips out to Rockaway Beach, in Queens, to "achieve the impossible," as the program's Web site puts it, "by standing on water."

The group departed from West Twenty-third Street on a recent Saturday morning. Unable to make the third outing,

Sachia's mentor, Dave Brennan—indisposed by one of the seven weddings he will attend this year—had arranged for three female volunteers to stand in for him. One of them, Sasha Shlyamberg, sought Sachia out on the sidewalk. (A photographer, Shlyamberg also bartends. "I tell the kids I waitress, though," she said.) "Hey, we're Team Sachia!" she told him. Sachia rolled his eyes and walked away.

An Alternative to Drugs and Violence

On the subway, a mentor in his late twenties assumed a surfer's stance as the train jerked from side to side. "Practicing balance," he said. Sunscreen was applied and passed around. A survey was handed out to the teenagers, with such questions as "During the last 30 days, how many times did you carry a gun?" and "During your life, how many times have you used marijuana?"

"Are you trying to get us arrested?" Sachia said.

Two subway transfers and a short walk later, the group had reached its destination: a five-hundred-yard stretch of beach that is the only spot in New York City designated for surfers alone. Close to eighty surfers bobbed on the four-foot swells.

Mentees rode in on their boards, some standing, many crouching, one lying face down with her eyes closed and her arms pressed against her sides.

A male volunteer said, "The mentees don't need to stretch, but we do."

First, though, some public service: a beach cleanup. Ten-odd members of a local environmental group were waiting on the beach when the Stoked crew arrived. They passed out latex gloves and garbage bags, and the pairs dispersed. Sachia followed several paces behind Shlyamberg and the two other women, a towel over his head. The haul included candy wrappers, straws, a pack of D batteries, a box of incense, a lime, several used condoms, a pack of cigarettes, and a silver spoon.

Learning to Have Fun

Finally, then, to the water! The mentees waded out first, each accompanied by an instructor, who helped acquaint them with their foam-top beginner boards and coached them on the finer points of "paddling hard and popping up." Sixteen-year-old Zaidy caught a wave and sprang to her feet. (Later, she said, "I've got natural talent, I guess," adding that two of her aunts, in Puerto Rico, are surfers.) Other mentees rode in on their boards, some standing, many crouching, one lying face down with her eyes closed and her arms pressed against her sides.

Sachia was the last one in the water. ("We had a hard time getting him to take his sneakers off the second week," a volunteer said.) His instructor, Joel Banslaben, explained that everyone's relationship with the water is different. "I want to stay in the white water," Sachia told him, referring to the area where he was able to stand. "That's fine," Banslaben said.

Following a morning of pointers, Sachia attempted to catch some waves close to shore. After a particularly triumphant ride, in which he coasted in with one arm raised, his pinkie and pointer finger extended to the sky, he undid his ankle leash and walked over to Shlyamberg, who was talking with another mentor by the water's edge.

"Did you see me pop up?" he said.

"Yeah! That was great!" Both women congratulated him, then resumed their conversation. "So I set my brother up with a friend of mine and he really likes her," Shlyamberg said.

"What? That's disgusting," Sachia said. "That means you're desperate and you can't get somebody on your own."

"That's not true," Shlyamberg said. Each woman gave him an example of a successful fix-up that she knew about.

Sachia looked out at the water. "I want to go back in," he said.

10

Deadly ATV Accidents in South Carolina Lead to Safety Legislation

Justin Anderson

Justin Anderson is a staff writer for the Charleston Daily Mail.

After fifty-four deaths related to ATVs in South Carolina during 2006, the State House is considering three bills that would enact stronger safety laws and ban ATVs from paved roads. The legislation, if passed, would require riders to wear helmets and register their vehicles with the state to obtain permits.

After a deadly year of ATV accidents in the state, three bills have been introduced in the House of Delegates to place safety restrictions on riders and require owners to register the vehicles with the state.

Fifty-four people died as a result of ATV crashes last year, with about half occurring on paved roads, according to the state Division of Motor Vehicles.

"The death rate has gotten way out of hand; to an unacceptable level," said Delegate Corey Palumbo, the lead sponsor of one of the safety bills. "I think for us to do nothing this year is unconscionable."

Two of the bills ... would ban ATVs from paved roads, following a recommendation from manufacturers and the State Police.

"I think the main issue is the paved road issue," Palumbo said today. He said it's a matter of the ATVs tires not being safe on pavement.

The bills also require riders of any age to wear helmets and bans additional passengers unless permitted by the ATV's manufacturer.

Keeping ATVs Off the Streets

[Delegate Kenneth] Tucker's bill orders state agencies to come up with an incident form that describes all known ATV accidents and orders the Division of Highways to include the forms in its annual traffic accident analysis.

Tucker's bill exempts the provisions of the law from riders legally operating ATVs in areas managed by the Hatfield Mc-Coy Regional Recreation Authority.

Riders going from trail to trail would only be allowed to ride on the berm of a main road for one mile, under Palumbo's bill. The law now says 10 miles.

"Ten miles is just an enormous distance when you're talking about going from one area of operation to another," Palumbo said.

Palumbo didn't have much hope for his bill's passage. But he's hoping it gets a discussion going.

"I think it's a situation where there's a big sentiment out in the state about letting people do whatever they want," he said.

"It's the 'Mountaineers are Always Free' mentality. I think that makes it difficult when you're trying to impose safety regulations of any kind."

Seeking Permission

Delegate Sam Argento, D-Nicholas, meanwhile, introduced a separate bill that would require owners and operators of ATVs to obtain off-road permit cards and display off-road identification on the ATV showing they have the permit.

Argento said around a half-million ATVs are estimated to exist in the state, but only about 150,000 are titled.

If the bill passes, all ATVs would have to be titled and a privilege tax paid by Oct. 1, 2008.

Under Argento's bill, people would pay a privilege tax when buying ATVs from a dealer or from a private owner. The tax is five percent of the value of the vehicle.

Argento said today that privilege tax collections on ATVs are hit or miss.

He said most dealers don't collect the tax unless the purchaser intends to have the ATV titled.

Paying for the Privilege to Ride

Applicants for the off-road permits and IDs would pay a $10 fee, and the documents would be good for the life of the ATV as long as it has the same owner.

Records of the applications would be forwarded on to county assessors for personal property tax collections.

The money collected from the permit applications would be deposited in a special account used to administer the permitting program.

Argento's bill also would make it a misdemeanor to violate the permitting process. A first offense could carry up to a $200 fine; second offense up to $500; and the third offense could mean a $1,000 fine and six months in jail.

He said one of the aims of his bill is to give law enforcement ways to identify troublesome riders of the ATVs in order to cite them for violations.

"Hopefully, this would cut down on that," Argento said.

11

Proposed ATV Age Restrictions Sparks Passions on Both Sides

Jeff Manning

Jeff Manning is a member of the Oregonian's *investigations team. He specializes in business crime and corruption.*

ATVs are involved in thousands of deaths and injuries annually, many of which affect children under the age of 16. In an attempt to lobby for age requirements for ATV riders and to enforce stricter ATV safety laws, one woman was met with great opposition. Susan Rabe, who lost her 10-year-old son in an ATV accident, was shocked when her proposal to ban anyone under 12 from riding ATVs sparked outrage from many ATV enthusiasts. These riders, who equate ATV riding with family fun and togetherness, were furious. They claimed that the death of Rabe's son came about not because ATVs are unsafe, but rather because of negligent parenting on Rabe's part.

After her 10-year-old son, Kyle, died on the family's all-terrain vehicle five years ago [in May 2002], Sue DeLoretto Rabe formed a group of moms who had lost kids on ATVs to push safety measures in Congress and states.

But it wasn't until the Turner woman tried to ban kids under 12 from ATVs in Oregon that things got ugly.

ATV proponents went on the attack. They called Rabe a negligent parent who contributed to her son's death. They dug

Jeff Manning, "Riders Throttle Safety Legislation," OregonLive.com, May 16, 2007. Republished with permission of *The Oregonian*, conveyed through Copyright Clearance Center, Inc.

up a police report about Kyle's accident. They mysteriously acquired a copy of the owner's registration Rabe signed when she bought her ATV that included her promise not to let anyone under 18 ride it.

Shocked and demoralized, Rabe quit the debate over "Kyle's Law" in March [2007].

"It really hurts to read these things," Rabe told the bill's supporters in an e-mail explaining her decision to drop out. "It brings everything back to the present."

Now, Kyle's Law appears dead in Salem, and only one of four other ATV safety bills at the Legislature has a chance. The reasons illustrate why states have proved a poor alternative to weak federal regulation of ATVs, which are involved in more than 800 deaths and 136,000 injuries a year. A quarter of the deaths and 30 percent of injuries are to children under 16.

Time and again, a vocal alliance of riders and ATV dealers has beaten back or watered down state legislation pushed by consumer advocates, trauma surgeons and bereaved parents.

For decades, the $5 billion-a-year ATV industry has advocated strict state laws on riding. But neither the ATV companies nor their trade group showed up in Salem this winter to support the safety bills, even though three of the measures were cribbed from the industry's "model legislation."

Officials at the industry's lobbying arm, the Specialty Vehicle Institute of America, said they knew about the Oregon bills but didn't come to testify in support of them because they weren't asked.

Who Should Regulate ATVs?

The ATV industry has fought regulation in Washington, D.C., for years by saying it's a job for the states.

But state ATV safety laws are a messy patchwork. A dozen states have no rules whatsoever. Others require helmets and training or set age limits, but the laws are rife with exceptions when riding on private lands or when a young rider is supervised by an adult.

During the past seven years, at least 30 children under age 16 died in ATV accidents in Oregon and Washington.

In Oregon, rider training and age limits are waived for a supervised child driving on public lands. Safety advocates say both ought to be mandatory to further ensure that children are kept out of danger, and they point out that the existing rules are lenient compared with those for cars and bicycles.

To get a driver's license in Oregon, teens must be at least 16 and pass written and skills tests. Kids under 16 are required to wear helmets to ride a bicycle. Not so to ride an all-terrain vehicle on private land in Oregon. A 6-year-old can hop aboard a 600-pound ATV that travels at freeway speeds and violate no law.

The results can be fatal. During the past seven years, at least 30 children under age 16 died in ATV accidents in Oregon and Washington. The toll includes Justin Burger, 7, of Scappoose and Austin Evers, 6, of Verboort, both of whom were driving adult-sized ATVs when they died after the vehicles rolled over.

The child deaths are among at least 162 ATV fatalities in the two states since 2000. More than 4,000 have been hospitalized with injuries.

As initially proposed, Kyle's Law would have banned anyone under 12 from riding ATVs on public or private lands. It quickly became a lightning rod for critics, who have dominated the ATV safety debate in Salem this year.

"It's Your Worst Fear"

Five years have passed since May 6, 2002, but the grief has not. Sue Rabe visits her son's grave regularly. On the headstone is an etching of Kyle atop the family's Arctic Cat 250.

Kyle and his friend Zach Rouse were riding ATVs that day. Kyle's ATV was not a youth model, but he rode as well as any adult, said his father, Tom Rabe. Traveling down a grassy slope, Kyle's machine overturned, pinning him to the ground. Though he wore a helmet and protective gear, he couldn't breathe under the ATV's weight.

Garth Rouse, alerted by his son, estimated he arrived at the scene 10 or 15 minutes after the accident. "By the time I got there, Kyle was gone, no breathing, no nothing," he said. "It's your worst fear that could ever happen."

The Rabes arrived minutes later and frantically started CPR. Tom Rabe said he could taste the milk and cookies Kyle ate at his friend's. An ambulance took Kyle to the hospital, but it was too late. He had died of asphyxiation [suffocation].

Numb with grief, the Rabes agonized over their role in Kyle's death and their naivete about the dangers of ATVs. When they bought the machine, their dealer sent an employee to "fit" the machine to Kyle, Sue Rabe said. No one questioned her son's age or size.

The Rabes never shirked their culpability in their son's death. The warning labels on the machine clearly stated that children under 16 shouldn't ride it.

"If someone blames me, I'll say, 'Yeah, it was my fault,'" Sue Rabe said.

Five months after the accident, Rabe took a call from Washington, D.C.

Rachel Weintraub, a lawyer who oversees product safety at the Consumer Federation of America, was searching for parents of children killed on ATVs. The federation advocated for a federal ban on sales of adult-sized ATVs for use by kids under 16, reasoning that it would send a stronger message to parents.

Weintraub told Sue Rabe that Kyle's death wasn't isolated—thousands of children had died on ATVs.

Rabe signed on. She did interviews with *People* and *Reader's Digest*. She heard from other mothers who'd lost children on ATVs. Eventually, she co-founded a group of mothers, Concerned Families for ATV Safety.

The similarity of the mothers' stories—the kids on adult-sized machines, the frequency of rollovers, the lack of awareness among parents that ATVs could kill—convinced Rabe that she was on the right track.

"I think this is what we were meant to do," she told her husband.

Cases Alarm Officials

Unbeknown to the Rabes, a handful of state officials also had ATVs on their radar.

At Oregon hospitals, ATV trauma cases had more than doubled over five years, reaching 414 by 2005. Treatment costs tripled to more than $12 million a year, and taxpayers bore nearly a quarter of the costs via Medicaid.

Separately, the Oregon Parks and Recreation Department compiled a report highlighting fatal ATV accidents. The usual three or four deaths a year had jumped to an average of 10 between 2000 and 2004. There were 13 fatalities in 2005 and 12 [in 2006].

The parks agency, which oversees off-road recreation on public lands, found that ATV riders were dying at nearly twice the rate of motorboat operators. The comparison seemed apt because the state had previously battled an increase in boat and personal watercraft fatalities—and won.

Personal watercraft, like ATVs, soared in popularity during the past 20 years. Better known by trade names such as Jet Ski, they accounted for eight deaths in the 1990s. In response, the Oregon Marine Board banned personal watercraft for anyone under 12 and required training and a written test for operators ages 12 to 17.

Since 1999, there has been just one personal watercraft fatality in Oregon.

If age limits and training worked for personal watercraft, parks officials reasoned, then why not for ATVs?

Finding a Middle Ground

But the issue put the department in a delicate position. The agency also promotes ATV riding in Oregon and is tightly allied with riders, spending millions of dollars for new off-road parks and trails. By law, a share of gas taxes is dedicated to off-road recreation. The department used the cash to build up a $21 million ATV fund.

Rabe and parks staffers talked about joining forces on a youth ATV ban. But the department didn't want to back age restrictions because they were so controversial among riders.

With 56,000 ATVs permitted for public lands, and thousands more operated on private property, Oregon's rider community was fertile ground for a rebellion against new regulation.

"I know that there are some safety advocates who want us to go further, but we decided only to go as far as we know the user community is supporting," parks official Kyleen Stone said in an internal e-mail *The Oregonian* obtained through a public records request, "They are a very effective lobby, so we would not get far if we opted to go beyond their stated levels of support."

In the end, the agency drafted four bills to govern ATVs on public lands. One would make helmets mandatory for all riders, not just those under 18. Another would prohibit passengers on machines designed for one rider. A third would require that ATVs be titled with the state, and the fourth would mandate training for all riders on public land.

The department's package seemed reasonable. All but the titling bill are advocated by the SVIA, the manufacturers' group. Plus, the committee of off-road enthusiasts that helps oversee the agency's ATV spending backed the bills.

Rabe took a different route.

She joined with Oregon SafeKids, a group of doctors, parents and public health officials, to push Kyle's Law. Several other states have adopted similar ATV age limits. The minimum in Maine is 10, in North Carolina, 8. The ATV industry says limits have helped reduce the share of child deaths as a portion of all ATV fatalities.

With Democrats controlling the Legislature and two of them—Sen. Richard Devlin of Lake Oswego and Sen. Alan Bates, a Medford physician—as lead sponsors, Rabe and her allies thought their chances looked good.

Soon, they were wondering what hit them.

Riders Fight Back

With 56,000 ATVs permitted for public lands, and thousands more operated on private property, Oregon's rider community was fertile ground for a rebellion against new regulation.

Many live in rural areas, and the issue carved a new fissure in the state's cultural divide.

Recreational riders equate ATV riding with family fun and togetherness. They were furious that the bill implied they were bad parents for letting their kids on ATVs. Others viewed the bills as more punishment for rural communities, akin to environmental rules that strangled the timber economy.

Some opponents of the bills struck an anti-government tone that reminded Bates of the gun control debate.

"They want to tax you, they want to regulate you, they want to get you off public lands," Rep. Greg Smith, R-Heppner, roared to a cheering crowd of ATV users who organized a pro-ATV rally at the Capitol in early February.

Others warned that small-town economies would suffer. Siuslaw National Forest officials figure half the 1.2 million annual visitors to the Oregon Dunes National Recreation Area come to ride ATVs and other off-road rigs.

DuneFest, a summer off-road event on the south coast, draws 10,000 riders a year. The Reedsport-Winchester Bay Chamber of Commerce estimates off-road recreation adds $10 million to the area economy.

[Pro-ATV lobbyists] repeated a common refrain: Riders who get hurt on ATVs are usually behaving irresponsibly.

"With the logging being where it's at and the salmon being where it is, we've got to be really grateful for the ATV industry," said chamber officer Joe Mirvis. "What is the next progression of industry for us? It's tourism and recreation. As far as the ATV industry, we've got to promote it."

The barrage of angry letters, e-mails and calls stunned the Kyle's Law sponsors.

Some were form letters orchestrated by off-road clubs. Others were impassioned, hand-scrawled pleas from riders arguing that ATVs were central to their lives and kept families together.

"I am turning 9 on April 14 and I LOVE riding quads," 8-year-old Jason Hector wrote to Devlin. "And if you prohibit this sport, I'll be very, very angry."

Temporary Insandity, an ATV club in Medford, threatened a recall drive against Bates.

"Get your phones and e-mails ready. . . this thing needs to go down in a flaming heap!" co-founder Patrick Bates said on the group's Web site.

The opposition bled over to the parks and recreation bills.

The Oregon Vehicle Dealers Association, headed by veteran lobbyist Monte King, condemned all five bills. Before a

House committee hearing, King repaeated a common refrain: Riders who get hurt on ATVs are usually behaving irresponsibly.

"You can't fix stupid," King said.

Lawmakers Soften Bill

Rider groups and dealers packed the February hearing, the first on the parks agency's package. By then, the fierce opposition had already given ATV safety proponents reason for pause.

In the Senate, Devlin's office collected more than 160 messages condemning Kyle's Law. Now on the defensive, he and Bates met to discuss ways to soften the bill. In the end, they agreed that the age limit should apply on public lands only. And rather than set the minimum age at 12, they lowered it to 8.

Rabe feared the senators might want to scrap the bill. But Devlin and Bates held firm.

Bates' resolve had been hardened by a chance encounter at his medical practice in Medford. The day that recall threats against him made local headlines, Bates was seeing patients. The first one was a man in his 20s who'd lost the use of his legs in an ATV accident at the dunes 10 years earlier.

Relieved that Kyle's Law still stood a chance, Rabe soon confronted another obstacle: her story.

Opponents circulated copies of the form she signed when buying the Arctic Cat, showing she checked boxes to waive free training and acknowledge it was an adult machine. ATV riders howled. Not only was Rabe a negligent parent, she was also a hypocrite in trying to shift blame from herself to the industry, they said.

Soon, they brandished the sheriff's report on Kyle's accident, which suggested that Kyle may have been pinned for an hour before the Rabes responded. The report is flatly contradicted by Garth Rouse, who was first to the scene. Nevertheless, the ATV enthusiasts used it to further vilify Sue Rabe.

How opponents got a copy of Rabe's ATV registration form remains a puzzle. Pat Richards, president and general manager of Fisher Implement, which sold the ATV to Rabe, said his company never provided it. Besides the Rabes, copies went to Arctic Cat and to the SVIA. Both denied making the form available.

Lindy Minten, a Scio mom and ATV enthusiast, emerged as a fierce critic of Kyle's Law and Sue Rabe, telling supporters at the Capitol that Kyle's death "wasn't a tragic accident. It was neglect and endangerment."

In an interview, Minten told *The Oregonian* the state has no business butting in on responsible parents. She continually brought the discussion back to the Rabes, saying that any parent who loses a child in an unsupervised ATV accident should be charged with negligent homicide.

"ATVs are dangerous," Minten said. "We need to make people aware of that, and we need to hold people accountable."

Mother Had Enough

By early March, the crush of flaming e-mails branding her a bad parent persuaded Rabe to drop out.

Kyle's Law never received a committee hearing. Legislators wanted no part of it.

The parks department bills to ban passengers and require vehicle titles never advanced. The helmet bill, once considered most likely to pass, went down 34-22 in the House. The measure calling for mandatory training remains alive, largely because of Minten's rider group, which supports hands-on courses rather than the Internet-based training that parks officials proposed.

Whether the ATV industry could have made a difference by testifying will never be known. The SVIA told parks officials it opposed Kyle's Law and has generally been leery of age limits. But since the 1980s, the trade group has called for mandatory training and helmet laws and a passenger ban—all identical to the parks department's bills.

Still, the SVIA never showed up.

"I don't think we were ever asked to come and testify," Kathy Van Kleek, the group's lead lobbyist, told *The Oregonian*. "I honestly don't recall."

Jim Myron, legislative coordinator for the parks department, said he underestimated the clout of riders.

Rabe, stung by the tactics of opponents, said she's done with Oregon politics for now.

"Does riding ATVs truly mean that much to them that they will do anything to discredit health officials, doctors and even the people who have lost a child?" Rabe said.

"No one is immune to this happening to them," she said of Kyle's death. "We never thought it could happen to us either, but it did. And you don't get a second chance."

12

Extreme Sports Can Have a Positive Impact on Life Outside the Arena

Arlo Eisenberg

Arlo Eisenberg is co-founder of Senate Wheels, an aggressive skating accessory manufacturer. He served as editor of Daily Bread *and was a gold medalist in the 1996 X Games.*

Sports have traditionally been viewed as a way for children to gain self-confidence and positive interpersonal relationships through teamwork, healthy competition, and victory. However, the growing popularity of extreme sports offers an opportunity to redefine the benefits of athletics as the emphasis of teamwork shifts to individual improvement and competing for a win becomes secondary to recreational enjoyment.

This is my disclaimer. This is your warning. Arrogance has been so stigmatized that it is difficult to be successful or confident without feeling guilty or feeling compelled to apologize for it. I am confident, I have been successful, I refer to myself in the third person as "The Arlo," and I ask friends and family to call me "god." I make no apologies. What follows is an egocentric observation on the state of rollerblading.

I was lucky to discover rollerblading before it had really caught on. Of course, rollerblading was lucky that I discovered it because I devoted my life to making sure that it caught on. Inline skating by itself already had a lot going for it; it was fast, fun, athletic, graceful, and easy to learn. On just its in-trinsic qualities alone, rollerblading would have gone far. It was destined to permeate every middle- to upper-class house-hold in the world. But I saw an even greater opportunity in rollerblading. As long as there was a vehicle that was capable of infiltrating mainstream culture on such a major scale, why not project some not so intrinsic qualities onto it and try to affect mainstream culture?

Rollerblading's timing couldn't have been better. It is in-credible, first of all, that an idea so inevitable as ice skating on dry land could have taken so long to come to market. After decades of suffering through clumsy, inefficient rollerskates, and despite the centuries that ice skating had been around and prospered, inline skates became available to the masses only at the end of the 1980s. By all accounts, this concept was as big as bicycles (how many households don't have at least one bicycle?), yet it managed to avoid materialization all the way until the end of the twentieth century. Ice skating on dry land was a predictable, logical evolution of human recreation and transportation, and thanks to the proliferation of paved roads and the development of polyurethane there was nothing to hold the idea back.

The Evolution of Rollerblading

Inline skates were released at the height of the media-saturated, trend-hungry, information age. Even bad ideas were able to prosper in this environment—remember those yellow signs hanging from car windows that read "Baby On Board" or "Jesus On Board," or "Baby In Trunk"? Imagine what would happen if you actually had not just a good idea, but a great one.

Inline skates landed on the world like a ton of bricks. It was a full-fledged phenomenon.

I predicted this. And I prepared for it.

By the time I discovered inline skates, when I was sixteen, I had already long since defined myself as a skateboarder. I was young and full of energy and aggression, so the physical act of skateboarding became my outlet for that. But what really drew me to skateboarding was its defiance. I loved how skateboarding was counterculture, how it criticized society and challenged convention—not just through the act of skateboarding, but by creating its own society, complete with its own language, its own music, and its own magazines. An entire culture evolved around the act of skateboarding.

Avoiding Previous Mistakes

Now skateboarding and its culture are indivisible. It is impossible to have one without the other. It is not enough to ride a skateboard to be a skateboarder—the culture of skateboarding is essential to its definition.

Some limitations of skateboarding were that it was so abrasive, and so antisocial, and it alienated itself so completely from the mainstream society that it made it near impossible to effect any kind of noticeable influence on any society other than its own. Also, aside from the abrasiveness of the culture, the actual act of skateboarding was very difficult, so it made it hard for people to be drawn to the scene in very large numbers.

People who are critical of rollerblading are always quick to point out that it is too easy. It is easier than skateboarding so it must rank lower than skateboarding in the mythical hierarchy of alternative sports, is the logic. It is my contention that accessibility is our greatest asset. When anyone says that rollerblading is too easy, they are actually saying that it is too easy to get into. It is impossible to measure rollerblading based on its limits because it is limitless. Everyone knows how to run, but that does not discount how difficult it is for Michael Johnson to run 200 meters in under twenty seconds. Just be cause something is easy to do does not necessarily mean that it is easy to take it to its extremes—it just means that you can take it further, quicker.

Through rollerblading we have the opportunity to take the ideals of all of the alternative sports to the world.

Unlike skateboarding, the rewards of rollerblading are immediate and consistent. The process of learning to skate on inlines is constantly gratifying so participants are encouraged to stick with it. Already rollerblading had one advantage built into it. But rollerblading was not skateboarding. There was no culture associated with it. It was just recreational activity. So what if the whole world started inline skating; what were the social ramifications of it? None.

Creating a Legend

Rollerblading—aggressive skating—was designed to be a mutation of skateboarding. The marriage of lifestyle to sport has been skateboarding's legacy and is a prerequisite to any contemporary action sport. Just like every other alternative sport before it and everyone after it, rollerblading took its cue from skateboarding. Unlike any other alternative sport, however, rollerblading has the unique opportunity to take the lifestyle/sport model to the masses.

The conventional wisdom in the unconventional circles of alternative sports is that acceptance by the mainstream is tantamount to death. My argument is that if we infiltrate the mainstream with new progressive ideas and change the mainstream, then we are doing society and ourselves a service. Through rollerblading we have the opportunity to take the ideals of all of the alternative sports to the world.

The social climate is ripe for new ideas. With the Cold War over and no real enemy to speak of, Saddam Hussein and Kenneth Starr notwithstanding, institutions designed to instill team values are no longer as relevant. Respecting authority and being a part of the team made sense when survival depended upon it, but in the absence of a universal evil to rally around, focus has moved away from the team and onto the individual. When it is a matter of life or death, there is a premium placed on winning; it is essential. If it is only a matter of life, then the premium is placed on more personal goals, such as enlightenment and gratification.

Changing the Definition of Success

Success is no longer measured in terms of team, or wins. Success is measured by how much the individual enjoys the experience. In the football model the individual trains diligently and receives instructions from the coaches, and the reward is in the team's victory, if it should have one, and in the discipline the individual receives (assuming society values discipline). In skateboarding or rollerblading the focus is not on competition, so the goal is not to win and the concept of training becomes obsolete. The reward is in the enjoyment the individual derives from the act of skating and in the camaraderie of the lifestyle.

The success of alternative sports is a testament to this new social environment. Children are deciding in growing numbers that they prefer action sports to the team-oriented sports that their parents played. More than any other action sport, rollerblading is prepared to accommodate this influx of new participants.

Without the advantage of decades of history to establish ourselves, we are the most malleable of all of the alternative sports.

Of all of the action sports, skateboarding, freestyle bmx, and rollerblading have the most mainstream potential because they can all be used for transportation and they can be used anywhere, unlike action sports such as surfing or snowboarding, which require an ocean or a mountain. Of all the "big three," rollerblading has the most mainstream potential because it is the easiest, and it has the most user-friendly image. Rollerblading's image is both an advantage and a liability, however.

A Culture Defined by Outsiders

Because rollerblading was new, we had the advantage of being able to review the action sports that came before us as we were attempting to define ourselves. We were able to borrow from what we thought were the best elements of the other action sports and we tried to steer clear of what we perceived to be weaknesses. In my vision, I wanted rollerblading to be rebellious. I wanted there to be an emphasis on the artistry of rollerblading as opposed to the athleticism. I valued style over difficulty. All of these qualities can be traced directly back to skateboarding. One thing that we tried to do differently, however, was to encourage as many people to participate in rollerblading as possible. We didn't want to undermine the built-in advantage of having such an accessible sport by making it an exclusive club like skateboarding.

For all of the advantages that our youth as a sport has afforded us, it has also been our biggest burden. Never mind the typical growing pains—the issues of credibility and acceptance from our peers will work themselves out over time. What we may not be able to recover from is the effect of the mainstream media on our identity. Without the advantage of decades of history to establish ourselves, we are the most malleable of all of the alternative sports. That fact, combined with the huge following rollerblading's unique accessibility has provided us, makes us a prime target for mainstream media eager to reach a new audience without losing an old one.

Since rollerblading was designed to infiltrate the mainstream, mainstream media is a necessary and valuable ally, but if the mainstream media is able to distort rollerblading's image to such a degree that it no longer represents the ideals it was designed to promote, then what is the value in the exposure? This dilemma has become the greatest challenge facing rollerblading.

As rollerblading's popularity grows, so do its pockets. Major sponsors eager to reach our coveted demographic are jumping in dollars first and they are making waves. The problem is not the sponsors or their money; we need them, in fact, if we want to grow. The problem is our age. Without a solid foundation to stand on, we always run the risk of caving in. When sponsors make suggestions or demands, without clearly defined parameters established through years of steady growth to fall back on, we are more susceptible to compromise. Compromise at a glance does not look like such a bad thing, but when it is compromise after compromise after compromise, eventually we run the risk of compromising away everything that we believed in. . . .

Reclaiming Our Values

Rollerblading is reaching the masses all right, but what is it saying? Who is controlling it? The answer is disturbing. We are letting our sport be defined by the people who have the things that we think we want. We have become consumed with our success, and are so eager to keep it going that we have lost sight of how we used to measure success.

The television producers are defining rollerblading now; the corporate sponsors are. Our parents are defining rollerblading. What was once an alternative to football is fast becoming a replacement for it. The focus in rollerblading is moving away from the personal goals of the individual and quickly moving toward winning championships and training to win championships.

How do we get it back? First we have to want it back. We have to want to change the world rather than want to be absorbed into it. We have to value innovation above athleticism. We have to be confident and arrogant. We have to make demands. We have to not be afraid of challenging convention, but committed to it. We must not be content. We must challenge. We must fight. No one knows better than we do what we want, so why let anyone else try to give it to us?

Organizations to Contact

The editors have compiled the following list of organizations concerned with the issues debated in this book. The descriptions are derived from materials provided by the organizations. All have publications or information available for interested readers. The list was compiled on the date of publication of the present volume; the information provided here may change. Be aware that many organizations take several weeks or longer to respond to inquiries, so allow as much time as possible.

Adventure Schools Rock Climbing
Springfield, VA   22150
(800) 39–CLIMB [392–5462] • fax: (703) 698–6114
e-mail: adventure@adventureschool.com
Web site: www.adventureschool.com

The ASRC is committed to providing personalized instruction in comprehensive climbing and safety. ARSC aims to help students become responsible, self-sufficient, and safe climbers.

American Bicycling Association (ABABMX)
PO Box 718, Chandler, AZ   85244
(480) 961–1903 • fax: (480) 961–1842
Web site: www.ababmx.com

The ABA establishes rules for BMX racing to provide family entertainment and fair competition. It promotes individual achievement and family support.

EXPN
c/o ESPN Television, Bristol, CT   06010
Web site: www.expn.go.com

EXPN is a division of ESPN dedicated to televised coverage of extreme sport events and athletes, particularly the annual summer and winter X Games.

International Association of Skateboard Companies (IASC)
22431 Antonio Pkwy., Ste. B160–412
Rancho Santa Margarita, CA   92688
(949) 455–1112 • fax: (949) 455–1712
Web site: www.skateboardiasc.org

IASC aims to promote skateboarding, increase participation, save members money through membership discounts, educate, and involve more youth in skateboarding.

International Surfing Association (ISA)
5580 La Jolla Blvd., PMB 145, La Jolla, CA   92037
(858) 551–5292 • fax: (858) 551–5290
e-mail: surf@isasurf.org
Web site: www.isasurf.org

The ISA is devoted to developing surfing, bodyboarding, and waveriding activities. ISA serves as the world's governing authority of these sports and offers guidance in the areas of competition, surf schools, and anti-drug education.

National Off-Highway Vehicle Conservation Council (NOHVCC)
427 Central Ave. West, Great Falls, MT   59404
(800) 348–6487 • fax: (406) 454–9142
Web site: www.nohvcc.org

NOHVCC represent off-highway vehicle manufacturers, dealers, and enthusiasts. The council promotes safe and responsible recreation through the use of all-terrain vehicles.

National Safe Boating Council (NSBC)
PO Box 509, Bristow, VA   20136
(703) 361–4294 • fax: (703) 361–5294
e-mail: NSBCdirect@safeboatingcouncil.org
Web site: www.safeboatingcouncil.org

The NSBC is a coalition for the advancement and promotion of safer boating through education. The council works with national and international leaders to improve development of boating safety educators for all water sports.

Stoked—Life Mentoring Through Action Sports
40 West 23rd Street, 2nd Floor, New York, NY   10010
(917) 262–3217 • (917) 262–3523
e-mail:losangeles@stokedmentoring.org
Web site: www.stokedmentoring.org

Stoked Mentoring is a non-profit organization that uses action sports to reach at-risk youth. The program aims to help teens develop into determined and successful citizens.

U.S. Olympic Education Center
Northern Michigan University, Marquette, MI   49855
(906) 227–2888 • fax: (906) 227–2848
Web site: http://webb.nmu.edu/SportsUSOEC

The USOEC provides educational opportunities for its resident athletes while offering world-class training. The Olympic Education Center is dedicated to preparing athletes to become Olympic champions. It offers support services to qualified athletes and coaches.

U.S. Parachuting Association (USPA)
5401 Southpoint Centre Blvd., Fredericksburg, VA   22407
(540) 604–9740 • fax: (540) 604–9741
e-mail: uspa@uspa.org
Web site: www.uspa.org

The USPA endorses safe skydiving with intensive parachute training, rating, and competition.

U.S. Ski and Snowboard Association
Box 100, 1500 Kearns Blvd., Park City, UT   84060
(435) 649–9090 • fax: (435) 649–3613
e-mail: info@ussa.org
Web site: www.ussa.org

It is the intention of the USSA to make U.S. athletes the best competitors in Olympic skiing and snowboarding. The mission of the USSA is to provide strong leadership that establishes and supports athletic excellence, integrity, teamwork, perseverance, loyalty, and accountability.

Bibliography

Books

Michael Bane   *Over the Edge: A Regular Guy's Odyssey in Extreme Sports.* Berkeley CA: Wilderness, 2000.

David Browne   *Amped: How Big Air, Big Dollars, and a New Generation Took Sports to the Extreme.* New York: Bloomsbury Publishing, 2005.

Coach Davies   *Xtreme Sports Training—Renegade Style.* St. Paul, MN: Dragon Door Publications, 2003.

Bruce Generaux   *Beyond the Comfort Zone: Confessions of an Extreme Sports Junkie.* Hanover, NH: Class Five, 2002.

Scott Graham   *Extreme Kids: How to Connect with Your Children Through Extreme (and Not So Extreme) Outdoor Sports.* Berkeley, CA: Wilderness, 2006.

Bear Grylls   *The Kid Who Climbed Everest.* Guilford, CT: Lyons, 2004.

Eddie Guerrero   *Cheating Death, Stealing Life: The*
and Michael   *Eddie Guerrero Story.* New York:
Krugman   Pocket Books, 2006.

Tim Hanna   *One Good Run: The Legend of Burt Munro.* New York: Viking Penguin, 2005.

Tony Hawk, with Sean Mortimer — *Hawk: Occupation: Skateboarder.* New York: ReganBooks, 2002.

Duncan Lennard — *Extreme Golf: The World's Most Unusual, Fantastic, and Bizarre Courses.* Naperville, IL: Sourcebooks, 2004.

Jeremy McGrath and Chris Palmer — *Wide Open: A Life in Supercross.* New York: HarperCollins Publishers, 2005.

Chris McNab — *Extreme Sports (Sports Injuries: How to Prevent, Diagnose, & Treat).* Broomall, PA: Mason Crest Publishers, 2004.

Rob Mundle — *Life at the Extreme: The Volvo Ocean Race Round the World 2005–2006.* Norwich, VT: Nomad, 2006.

Patricia Oudit — *Snowboarding.* Fitway Publishing, 2006.

Gary Paulsen — *How Angel Peterson Got His Name: And Other Outrageous Tales About Extreme Sports.* New York: Wendy Lamb Books, 2003.

Paul Stanton — *Extreme(ly Dumb) Sports.* Hamilton, MT: Duckboy Cards, 2004.

Peter Stark — *Last Breath: The Limits of Adventure.* New York: Random House Publishing, 2002.

Andrew Todhunter — *Dangerous Games: Ice Climbing, Storm Kayaking, and Other Adventures from the Extreme Edge of Sports.* New York: Doubleday, 2000.

Joe Tomlinson	*Extreme Sports: In Search of the Ultimate Thrill.* London: Carlton Books, 2004.
Joe Tomlinson	*Ultimate Encyclopedia of Extreme Sports.* London: Carlton Books: 2002.

Periodicals

Patricia Leigh Brown	"This Is Extremely Sporting," *New York Times*, August 13, 2000.
Brad Buxton	"Extreme Sports," *Combat Edge*, August 2003.
Brian Handwerk	"Fear Factor: Success and Risk in Extreme Sports," *National Geographic News*, July 9, 2004.
Jack Howard	"X-Rated Surfing?" *Surfer*, April 2003.
Gwen Kilvert	"Missing the X Chromosome," *Sports Illustrated Women*, July 1, 2002.
Lori Balance Laird	"Cool Moms, Safe Kids," *Los Angeles Family Magazine*, 2006.
Tim Layden	"What Is This 34-Year-Old Man Doing on a Skateboard? Making Millions." *Sports Illustrated*, June 10, 2002.
Brian MacPherson and Richard O'Brien	"The X Games Ramp It Up in Los Angeles," *Sports Illustrated*, August 1, 2005.
Vicki Michaelis	"White Gliding in Gold Afterglow," *USA Today*, January 24, 2007.

Joan Raymond   "Going to Extremes," *American De-mographics*, June 1, 2002.

Selena Roberts   "Some Winter Stars Prefer Green to Gold," *New York Times*, February 7, 2002.

Andrew Romano   "Paintball Passions," *Newsweek*, March 19, 2007.

Sal Ruibal   "X Games Upstarts Now Embrace the Olympics," *USA Today*, January 26, 2006.

Jon Saraceno   "Long-retired Daredevil Frail, Feisty, Still Cheating Death," *USA Today*, January 3, 2007.

Jill Steeg   "New Thrills—and Spills—at X Games," *USA Today*, August 2, 2006.

Scott Willoughby   "Embracing Extreme Snowboarding Evolves into Darling of Olympic Games," *Denver Post*, February 10, 2006.

Mike Wise   "Skateboarders Are Landing in Real World," *New York Times*, August 18, 2002.

Craig C. Young,   "Extreme Sports: Injuries and Medi-
M.D.,   cal Coverage," *Current Sports Medicine Reports*. Current Science, Inc., 2002.

Glen Zorpette   "Extreme Sports, Sensation Seeking and the Brain." *Scientific American*, May 1, 2002.

| Marvin Zuckerman | "Are You a Risk Taker?" *Psychology Today*, November–December 2000. |

Index